£12.99

CONTENTS

SYCO tv

talkback THAMES

FREMANTLEMEDIA

Pedigree®

Published 2011. Pedigree Books, Beech Hill House,
Walnut Gardens, Exeter, Devon, EX4 4DH.
books@pedigreegroup.co.uk | www.pedigreebooks.com
Written by Rachel Elliot | Photographs © FremantleMedia Limited.
Pedigree Books would like to thank Cat Lawson and
Caren Davies for their help in compiling this book.

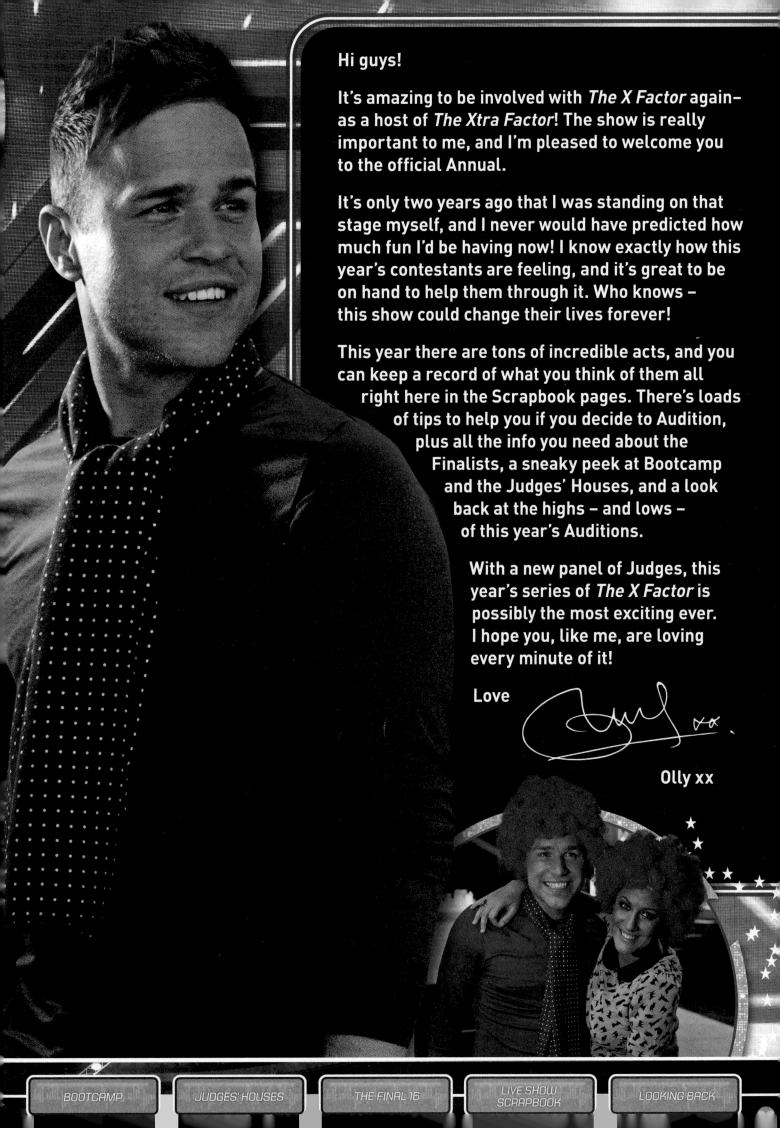

Hi guys!

It's amazing to be involved with *The X Factor* again – as a host of *The Xtra Factor*! The show is really important to me, and I'm pleased to welcome you to the official Annual.

It's only two years ago that I was standing on that stage myself, and I never would have predicted how much fun I'd be having now! I know exactly how this year's contestants are feeling, and it's great to be on hand to help them through it. Who knows – this show could change their lives forever!

This year there are tons of incredible acts, and you can keep a record of what you think of them all right here in the Scrapbook pages. There's loads of tips to help you if you decide to Audition, plus all the info you need about the Finalists, a sneaky peek at Bootcamp and the Judges' Houses, and a look back at the highs – and lows – of this year's Auditions.

With a new panel of Judges, this year's series of *The X Factor* is possibly the most exciting ever. I hope you, like me, are loving every minute of it!

Love

Olly xx

Olly xx

MEET THE JUDGES
GARY BARLOW

GARY'S PROFILE

The front man of the biggest boy band on the planet has written some of the best-known songs in pop. Now he faces a brand-new challenge as a Judge on the biggest show on TV.

Gary has had twelve UK number-one hits and has received the Ivor Novello award for songwriting five times. He taught himself to play the keyboard when he was a child, and in his teens he reached the semi-finals of a BBC songwriting competition. He went on to perform on the club circuit, before a casting agent put him together with four other guys to form Take That.

"There's only one goal – to find a SUPERSTAR."

The members of Take That have become pop legends, and they all actively support new talent. Having been a fan of *The X Factor* for several years, Gary jumped at the chance to help find the next superstar. He vividly remembers how he felt when he started out in the music industry, and he is looking forward to helping other young people to follow in his footsteps.

As a Judge, Gary is looking for passion, personality and stage-presence, as well as the X factor, of course!

"I am so EXCITED to be a Judge on *The X Factor*."

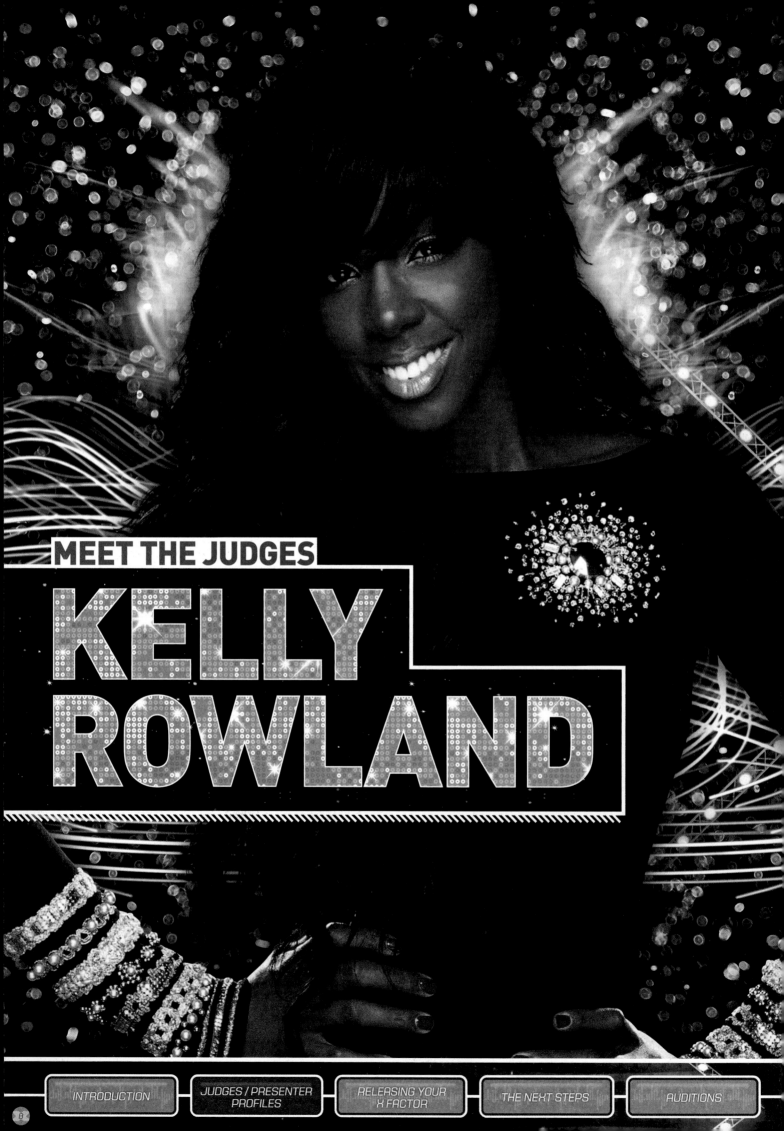

MEET THE JUDGES
KELLY ROWLAND

KELLY'S PROFILE

Bringing a taste of America to the show, Kelly joined the Judging panel hoping to discover new talent. She is looking forward to developing the abilities of the contestants and guiding them towards becoming real recording artists.

Kelly has been working in the music industry since a young age. She was one of the founding members of Destiny's Child, alongside Beyoncé. The band has sold over sixty million records, and Kelly has also become a Grammy Award winning solo star.

"I'm INSPIRED by the talent I see."

Since her solo career started in 2002, she has sold over four million albums and eighteen million singles. But Kelly likes to be busy, and she has also tried her hand at acting, with appearances in sitcoms and films.

When the Audition process began, Kelly knew exactly what she was looking for. She wanted to see passion, hunger and worldwide appeal. She's looking forward to nurturing the acts in her category – and she's also having a blast getting to know the UK better!

"This show could change your life FOREVER"

MEET THE JUDGES
TULISA

TULISA'S PROFILE

Tulisa may be the youngest ever *X Factor* Judge, but she has bags of experience to help her out!

She's been the lead singer of Britain's biggest hip-hop band since she was a teenager. With nine hit singles, four Mobo awards and two platinum albums, she is a perfect choice for the Judging panel.

At first Tulisa was a solo performer, but then Dappy and Fazer asked her to be part of their band and they started to perform together. They followed their dream for years, performing around

"This is about finding something FRESH."

Camden, so Tulisa knows how hard musicians have to work to get a break. Her experience as a young musician helps her relate to the young contestants she sees on the show.

Tulisa is still working with Fazer and Dappy, and N-Dubz is more popular than ever before! She'll be encouraging the acts in her category to make the most of the opportunity to sing in front of a live audience.

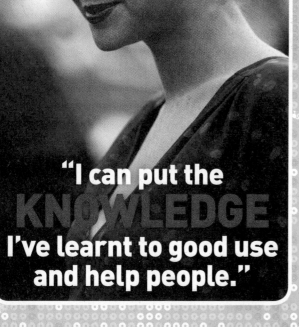

"I can put the KNOWLEDGE I've learnt to good use and help people."

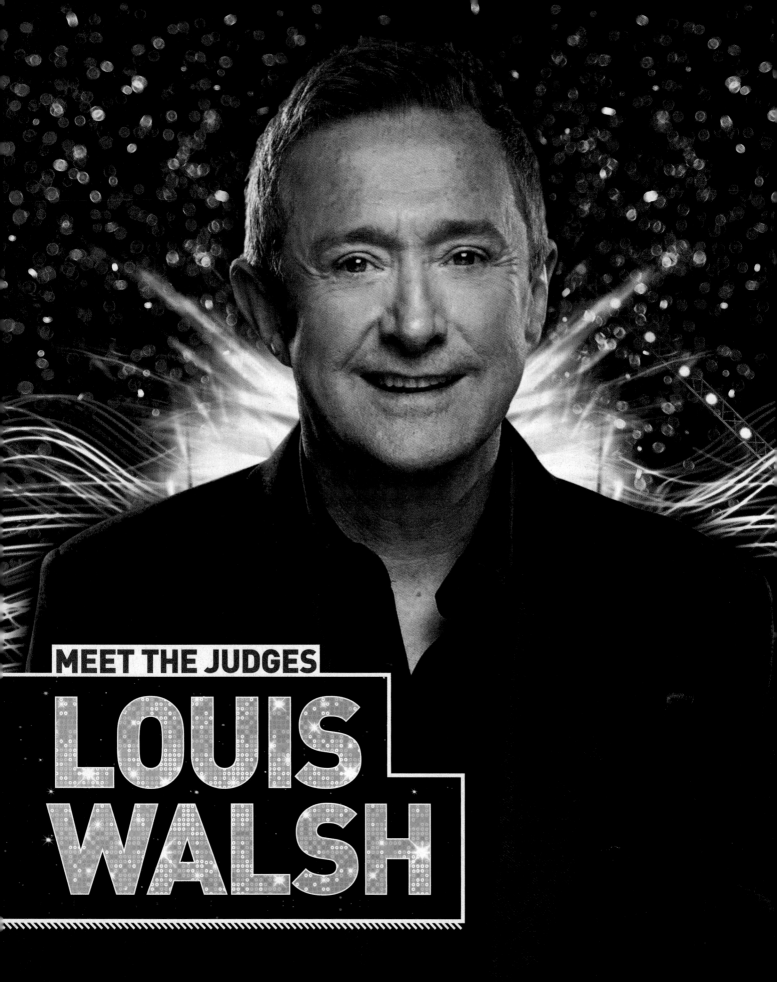

MEET THE JUDGES
LOUIS WALSH

LOUIS' PROFILE

The only original Judge is back, and he can't wait to discover the best talent of 2011!

Louis is well known for his enthusiasm and sense of fun, but don't forget that he is also the man behind some of the most successful bands in pop history. He has masterminded the careers of Boyzone, Westlife and Girls Aloud.

He first showed his talent for picking pop stars when he spotted an artist called Johnny Logan. Louis persuaded him to sing at The Eurovision Song Contest and, when Johnny won, his first album sold half a million copies within three days of its release.

Louis has helped Boyzone achieve sixteen top-three singles and four number-one albums, selling over twelve million copies worldwide. He guided Westlife to thirteen UK number ones and six number-one albums.

"It's really the **MOST FUN** I've ever had filming the show."

He has proved his skills as a talent spotter and manager time after time, mentoring such stars as Ronan Keating, Jedward, G4 and *The X Factor* winner Shayne Ward. He is skilled at recognising an act the public will love, and he is always passionate about contestants who genuinely love music.

With three new Judges beside him, Louis' experience is invaluable to the show. Will 2011 be the year that Louis triumphs again?

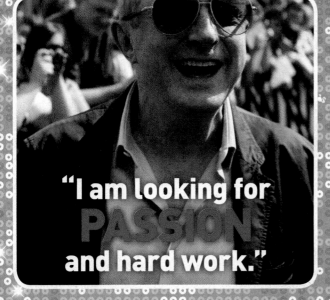

"I am looking for **PASSION** and hard work."

CAROLINE FLACK

CAROLINE'S PROFILE

Presenting *The Xtra Factor* alongside Olly Murs has to be one of the most desirable jobs in the UK, and Caroline Flack couldn't be more excited.

"Filming the show so far has been a blast. Olly and I are having so much fun meeting all the contestants. It's a roller-coaster ride of emotions and you can feel the nerves in the atmosphere."

Caroline has already achieved plenty during her amazing TV career. She's managed to stay cool under the threat of poisonous insects on *I'm A Celebrity, Get Me Out of Here!* Now, as well as thrashing her competitors on ITV2's *Minute To Win It* and holding court on the red carpet of *The Brits*, she's battled *Gladiators* for Sky One and thrown serious shapes on BBC1's *Let's Dance For Comic Relief*. Phew! Sounds like Miss Flack is more than ready to face the music on this year's *Xtra Factor*!

"Louis Walsh is always making everyone laugh, he's a joy to be around."

Caroline has loved watching the Auditions from inside the arenas, and giving you all the exclusive backstage access to *The X Factor* gossip. As a long-term fan of the show, she's looking forward to seeing some fireworks as the competition heats up. But what's her hot tip for who will win *The X Factor*?

"I do think it will be the year of the girls . . ."

Already building quite a reputation for her style, Caroline's attitude and sense of fun make *The Xtra Factor* a show you can't afford to miss!

DID YOU KNOW? | Caroline is a twin!

INTRODUCTION | JUDGES / PRESENTER PROFILES | RELEASING YOUR X FACTOR | THE NEXT STEPS | AUDITIONS

OLLY'S PROFILE

Olly is new to presenting *The Xtra Factor*, but he's way more familiar with the show than your average fresh-faced presenter! In 2009 he made it all the way to *The X Factor* Final, and since then he has released several chart-topping singles and a fantastic first album.

When he first appeared on *The X Factor*, Olly was working as a customer advisor and could only dream of being a pop star. But his fantastic Audition made him an instant hit with the audience and the Judges, and soon he was on the road to fame.

Fast forward two years, and Olly's whole life has changed. He's had two number-one singles, a double platinum album, and now he's taking up a new role as a presenter. A few things have changed on the show since he competed, but the contestants are just as nervous as ever!

"Making an impression for those few minutes at Auditions and the Live Shows is so important."

One thing's for sure – Olly is able to support this year's acts in a way that no other presenter can. He understands how it feels to stand in the wings with a pounding heart and shaking legs, and he's always there to remind the contestants to keep their eyes on the prize. After all, he knows first-hand that this show can make dreams come true.

"It can literally change your life."

DID YOU KNOW?

Olly loves football and played semi-professionally for Witham Town F.C.

MEET THE PRESENTERS
OLLY MURS

DERMOT O'LEARY

DERMOT'S *PROFILE*

Dermot is the presenter of *The X Factor*, he is the friendly face of the show, and he's on hand to support the acts from the first Audition right through to the Live Final. He plays the crucial role in *The X Factor*, acting as the bridge between the Judges, the audience and the contestants.

Dermot began his career as a researcher and went on to establish T4 for Channel 4. He's a massive music fan and spends Saturday afternoons presenting his own show on BBC Radio 2. He gets a huge kick out of being the presenter of the biggest show on TV, and he's really excited about this year's new judging panel.

"The new judges are terrific. They hit the ground running from the very start."

Dermot won't reveal his fave contestants, but he watched every Audition and helped to guide the contestants through Bootcamp and Judges' Houses. So which category does he think has the best chance of making the Final?

"The girls are really strong. They've really over achieved this year."

DID YOU KNOW?

Dermot likes the Auditions, Bootcamp and Judges' Houses, but he loves the Live Shows best. He looks forward to Saturdays and Sundays every week!

RELEASE YOUR X FACTOR!

You've watched other people stand up on that famous stage, and you've dreamed that one day it might be you. Well now it's time to stop daydreaming and turn your fantasy into reality!

To be successful at Auditions, shine at Bootcamp and dazzle at Judges' Houses, you need to make sure that you stand out from the crowd. It's vital to put in the work and prove to the Judges that you are determined to follow your dream.

In the next few pages, you'll find your very own 'How To' guide to finding the X factor inside you. What's your hidden skill? What image and sound will best suit your personality? Use this guide to find and develop your unique talents.

BECOMING A SUPERSTAR STARTS RIGHT HERE!

FINDING HIDDEN SKILLS

When you turn up for your *X Factor* Audition, the Judges will be looking for your USP.

Unique Selling Point

So what is special and new about you? The Judges might ask, so make sure that you have your answer prepared.

You should also think about what you can do to help yourself stand out from the crowd. The Judges and the audience see many Auditionees each day, so you need to make sure that they remember you – even when they've seen hundreds of other acts!

THE SOUND

Of course, it's with your voice that you can most impress the Judges. If you have a tone or style that blows them away, it could be all the USP you need. Some of these performers were shy, nervous or awkward at their first Auditions, but their star quality shone through.

Janet Devlin

Stacey Solomon
Series 6

Leona Lewis
Series 3

Rebecca Ferguson
Series 7

Olly Murs
First Audition
Series 6

MUSICAL SKILLS

Can you play an instrument? Many successful singers are also talented musicians. Pick your favourite instrument and think about getting some lessons.

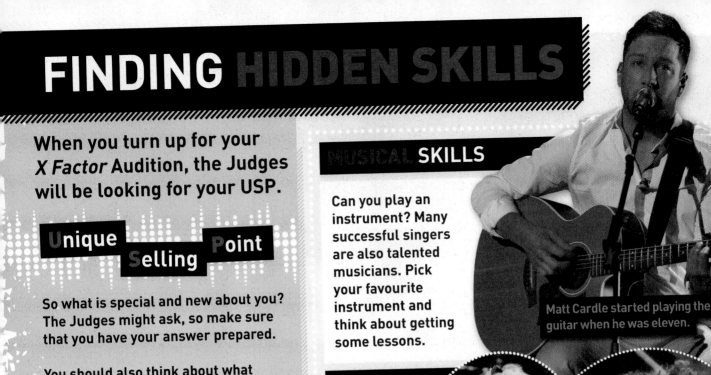
Matt Cardle started playing the guitar when he was eleven.

THE HAIR

There have been some weird, wonderful and totally wild hairstyles on the show. A great hairstyle can make you unforgettable, but remember that there's a fine line between fabulous and frightful!

Katie Waissel
Series 7

Nathalie Makoma

Mark Byron

Sophie Bond

Chelsea Sianga

THE FASHION

Your image can tell the Judges and the audience a lot about your style and your music. Check out these pics – what sort of music do you think these singers perform? You can choose to use other artists for inspiration, or you could create a brand-new look for your brand-new sound!

Misha Byran

Randy Roxx

Coralie Jo

THE MOVEMENT

Being a performer isn't all about your voice. You have to be able to move around the stage with confidence, and know how to work the audience. If you can give a full performance at your Audition, you will show the Judges that you would make a great choice for the Live Shows.

RELEASING YOUR X FACTOR!

FASHION

Your appearance will have the Judges and the audience evaluating you as soon as you walk onstage, so you will want to look your best. *The X Factor's* head fashion stylist and costume designer has some tips to help you decide on an outfit that reflects your personality!

X FACTOR'S FASHION X-PERT

The X Factor's head fashion stylist and her team of six assistants style all the contestants, as well as the dancers and the bands for the Live Shows. She works with the creative teams to decide on a visual concept for each performance.

2 Shoes

What fashion mistakes should Auditionees avoid?

Don't have too much going on. I am all about eclectic and thrown together, but when someone puts too many trends in the same look, it's as if the clothes are wearing them instead of vice versa!

How should an Auditionee start putting their image together?

First and foremost, think about your body shape and which cuts and styles work for you. Then think about the market you want to appeal to and which genre you fit into.

Boy v Girl

Edmar Teixeria

Becky Shaw

Chess Leigh

Gemma McDowell

What styles are you loving at the moment?

Forties and fifties themes are on trend for autumn. Print and floral are also big. There's a lot of bright colour-blocking and vibrancy, houndstooth and checks, but these styles aren't the easiest looks to wear! Clothing is definitely more structured than in past seasons.

"Working on *The X Factor* is a hubbub of CREATIVITY and FUN!"

Misunderstood

How would you style a band?

It's important to look like a band – you need to be cohesive and show that you fit together. Think about your music and looks to help you choose a style direction. That direction could be a trend, a style or a colour, but you can use it to tie the group together.

Dolled Up

1 Direction
Series 7

Which past Auditionees have stood out for you?

Cher Lloyd was super-cool in her initial Audition. She was rocking a fantastic street look when she sang for the first time.

Cher Lloyd
Series 7

What is the best part of your job?

As a stylist, the best part of my job is working with incredibly talented people from artists through to photographers and fashion designers. One of the biggest highs is seeing my work aired on TV, in pop videos and on artists' world tours.

I also get to travel the world, and have worked in places as diverse as Alaska, the Ukraine, Rio and Udaipur.

I've worked with a long list of celebrities and artists from Lady Gaga and Britney Spears to Kanye West and Usher. But *The X Factor* will be different, because I will be creating looks for potential new stars that will define who they are as artists.

X-CLUSIVE EXPERT TIP:

You should think about what will look good on camera. Choose solid primary colours or black. Be careful of prints, especially geometric, because they may pixilate on screen. White can also be tricky.

John Adams

X-CLUSIVE EXPERT TIP:

I think it's important to be a style chameleon at the Audition stage. Don't get too fixed on any particular look!

Ben Dillan

Lillie Laverick

"MY INSPIRATION comes from fashion shows, magazine shoots, music videos and art."

HOW TO STYLE A MALE VOCALIST

There are a few key looks that tend to work well for most male artists.

SKINNY SUITS

Andrew Grogan

but the guy needs to be skinny!

STREET LOOK

Ian 'IKA' Crossfield

good jeans, cool trainers and a fantastic leather bomber.

SKATER BOY LOOK

Eskimo Smile

skinny jeans and a lumberjack shirt.

PREPPY LOOK

John Prichard

ankle-skimming trousers and a shirt buttoned to the top.

Bigger-sized guys should stick to dark colours and simple styling – black, for example, with no prints.

HOW TO PUT TOGETHER A ROCK CHICK LOOK

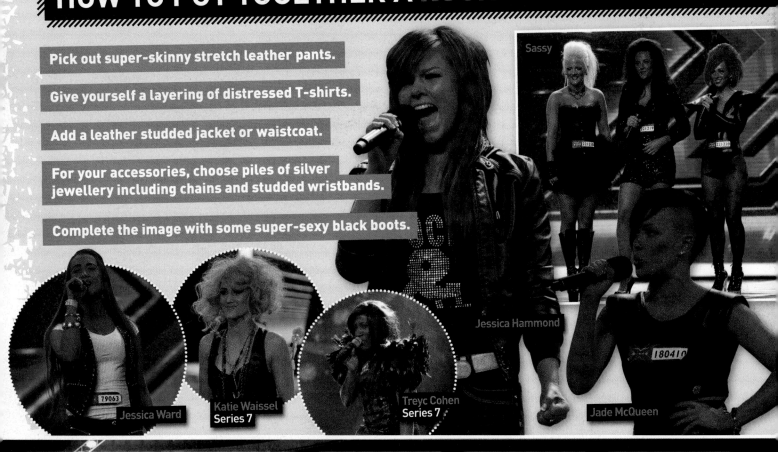

Pick out super-skinny stretch leather pants.

Give yourself a layering of distressed T-shirts.

Add a leather studded jacket or waistcoat.

For your accessories, choose piles of silver jewellery including chains and studded wristbands.

Complete the image with some super-sexy black boots.

Sassy

Jessica Hammond

Jessica Ward

Katie Waissel
Series 7

Treyc Cohen
Series 7

Jade McQueen

RELEASING YOUR X FACTOR!

MAKE-UP

It's vital that you look and feel your best when you turn up for your Audition. When you're facing the Judges and thousands of *X Factor* fans, you'll want to feel confident about your appearance. But don't worry; *The X Factor's* Head Make-up Artist has plenty of hints and tips to enable you to look like a pop star!

X FACTOR'S MAKE-UP X-PERT

The X Factor's Head Make-up artist works on the Live Shows to create individual looks for the artists. She helps each Finalist to develop their image, as well as designing make-up to match each song and performance.

What's the best skincare routine for girls?

Always remove your make-up at night! Your skin repairs itself while you're sleeping, so if you leave on cloggy make-up you'll block your pores and have a rough complexion. In the morning, cleanse, tone and moisturise. Repeat this routine before you go to bed.

What's the best skincare routine for guys?

Firstly, chuck out the soap you use on your face! It strips the skin of its natural oils and creates more spots because the skin balance has been disrupted. Instead, use a gentle face wash. Finish off with a light, oil-free moisturiser and boom! You're ready to go!

X-CLUSIVE EXPERT TIP

Older contestants should stay away from shimmer and powder products and dark lips – they enhance lines! Use coral colours and cream eyeshadows and blush.

Have you got any advice for male Auditionees?

Matte down your face. I see so many contestants with a shiny forehead that says hello to the Judges before they do! Just use a simple mattifying face cream – you can get it from your local chemist.

What are your tips for female Auditionees?

Keep your make-up nice and simple. Imagine that you are going to meet your boyfriend's mum for the first time! Wear very little foundation – none at all if you can. Touch up any blemishes with concealer and dust with a clear translucent powder. Add simple eyeliner and a clear lip-gloss and away you go!

Who was your favourite past contestant in terms of image and why?

I love Matt Cardle's rough-and-ready look – it's so nice and natural. Among the girls I think Rebecca Ferguson is amazing! Her make-up is so elegant and simple . . . just beautiful. She looked elegant, sexy and – most importantly – herself.

How do you create a look for a band?

First I look at their style and hair, and then I think about the type of music they sing. It varies massively from artist to artist!

How does being on camera affect make-up?

Make-up works very differently in front of a camera. The camera lens enhances your face, and the lights around suck up the colour of your skin. Therefore colours need to be stronger than for everyday make-up.

How should an Auditionee start to decide on a look?

Turn on your TV and look at how the people you like do their make-up. Check out your fave singers too, but don't go extreme like Lady Gaga.

What's your favourite make-up trend?

At the moment it's the creative eyeliners everyone's doing. I love it!

X-CLUSIVE EXPERT TIP

One huge mistake that people make all the time is over-the-top make-up. Mascara, gloss, lashes . . . and too much orange fake tan! Ugh! Another big mistake is forgetting to use powder. Shiny faces everywhere!

What's the most fun aspect of working in make-up?

I love creating a look for a fresh-faced artist. It's great seeing the transformation. It's all about making people feel better about themselves.

Which stars' make-up do you like?

I'm loving Jessie J's make-up at the moment, as well as Nicki Minaj and – of course – Adele! Elle MacPherson always looks fresh and immaculate.

HEAD MAKE-UP ARTIST GUIDE
TO A NATURAL LOOK

FOR THIS MINIMALIST LOOK YOU WILL NEED SHORT NAILS OR A SMALL SHADOW BRUSH OR SPONGE TIP APPLICATOR.

1. Lightly apply oil-free moisturiser all over your face.

2. Use a little concealer, but only where and if you need it – on red spots or under your eyes, for example. Blend it in with your fingers.

3. Now apply a very light tinted moisturising foundation all over your face and blend outwards with your fingertips.

4. Using your fingertips, dot pink cream blush onto the apples of your cheeks.

5. Your eyebrows should be groomed. Tweeze any stray hairs or book an appointment at a beauty salon if you're not sure where to start. Fill in bare spots with strokes of a brow pencil closest to your own colour. Brush the hairs together going up and outwards.

6. Using your fingertips, dab shimmery white eyeshadow into the inside corners of your eyes.

7. Keep your eyelids looking fresh with a dab of colour closest to your skin colour.

8. Next, curl your lashes. Always lift your eyebrows with a finger and look down when using the eyelash curler.

9. Apply a thin coat of black mascara (or dark brown if you are blonde) to the top lashes. Forget the bottom lashes as the mascara will run or flake and make you look too made up.

10. Define the natural shape of your lips and fill them in using a light pink or natural-colour lip pencil.

11. Finally give your lips a sweep of sheer gloss and blot slightly.

X-CLUSIVE EXPERT TIP

My big make-up tip for 2012 is COLOUR! That's what I'll be thinking about for the contestants this year. Colour, colour, colour. There's no need to be afraid any more!

VOILA – NATURAL BEAUTY!

HEAD MAKE-UP ARTIST GUIDE
TO A ROCK CHICK LOOK ....

MY VERSION OF THIS CLASSIC MAKE-UP WILL GIVE YOU A WET, SMOKY-EYED LOOK, WHICH IS REALLY DRAMATIC FOR THE STAGE!

1. Prepare your skin with an oil-free moisturiser.

2. If needed, apply concealer to match your skin tone and blend well.

3. Lightly groom your eyebrows and fill them in where needed with a brow pencil that matches your own colour.

4. Take a soft-tipped black eye pencil and apply a line to the inner rim of the eye, top and bottom. Smudge onto the lash line.

5. Using a shadow brush, apply a basic black powder eyeshadow. Start at the outer corner of your eye and work towards the inner corner. Keep blending and smoothing all along until you have covered the whole lid.

6. Now use a black cream eyeshadow or liquid liner to deepen the black. Go over the whole lid and slightly underneath the lash line. Don't worry if it's messy – it's part of the look!

7. Apply petroleum jelly across the eyelids. You can use a shimmery silver colour on top.

8. Curl your lashes and enhance with black mascara top and bottom.

9. Using your fingertips, blend a little soft pink cream blush onto your cheeks.

10. Line and fill in your lips with a natural-colour lip pencil, then sweep with a sheer red lip gloss.

X-CLUSIVE EXPERT TIP

Sort out your eyebrows professionally at a salon. It can lift years off you and enhance your features, so it's very important!

BOOM! NOW YOU'RE READY TO ROCK OUT!

RELEASING YOUR X FACTOR!

The X Factor is a singing competition, which means that your vocals have got to be good. You can change your image and you can learn cool dance moves, but if you don't have the raw talent then you are never going to reach Bootcamp. Luckily technical vocal coach Anne-Marie Speed is on hand with some great advice!

VOCALS

ANNE-MARIE
X FACTOR'S VOCALIST X-PERT

Anne-Marie works with the Finalists to help them polish and develop their voices, and to prepare for the daunting live performances.

Contestants at Bootcamp

What is your role on The X Factor?

I worked with the contestants on the last day of Bootcamp – just before they went to Wembley Arena. It was my job to listen to them singing and make sure that they were not sounding too tired. I also checked that they had made a good song choice, and that they were singing in the right key.

During the Live Shows, I help the contestants to understand their voices from a technical point of view. I aim to make it easier for them to perform.

Contestants at Bootcamp

John Wilding

Do you prefer to work with contestants who have had vocal training?

It depends on the training! Some training can be unhelpful. The best contestants are the ones who are open and enthusiastic.

Amelia Lily

What should a potential Auditionee know about improving their voice?

It is massively important to find a teacher who really understands how the voice works, and how the body functions. I use the Estill model for training, which is based on an understanding of function. The voice is muscular and it has rules, and teaching is easier when you understand that.
Visit www.thevoiceexplained.com for more information.

The Keys

Jade Richards

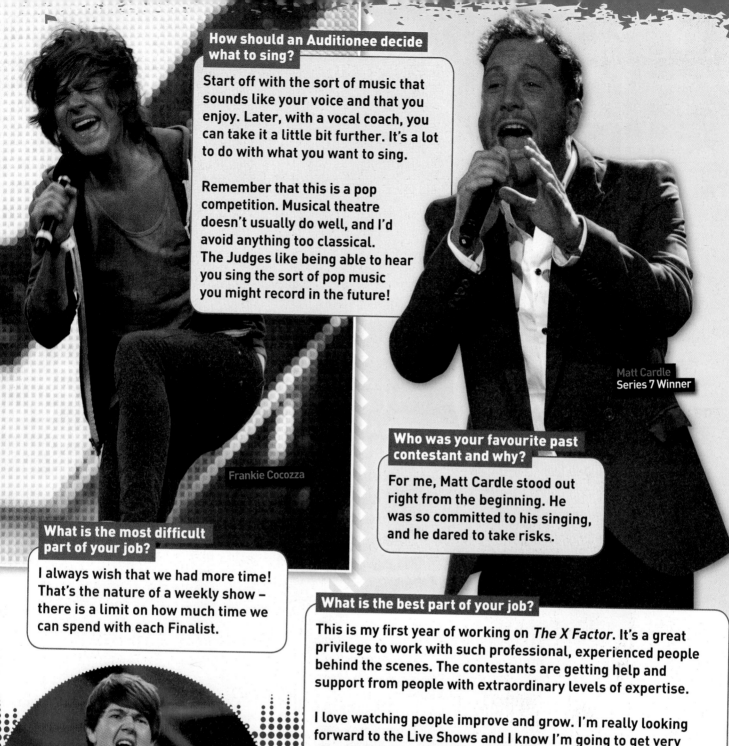

How should an Auditionee decide what to sing?

Start off with the sort of music that sounds like your voice and that you enjoy. Later, with a vocal coach, you can take it a little bit further. It's a lot to do with what you want to sing.

Remember that this is a pop competition. Musical theatre doesn't usually do well, and I'd avoid anything too classical. The Judges like being able to hear you sing the sort of pop music you might record in the future!

Frankie Cocozza

Matt Cardle
Series 7 Winner

Who was your favourite past contestant and why?

For me, Matt Cardle stood out right from the beginning. He was so committed to his singing, and he dared to take risks.

What is the most difficult part of your job?

I always wish that we had more time! That's the nature of a weekly show – there is a limit on how much time we can spend with each Finalist.

What is the best part of your job?

This is my first year of working on *The X Factor*. It's a great privilege to work with such professional, experienced people behind the scenes. The contestants are getting help and support from people with extraordinary levels of expertise.

I love watching people improve and grow. I'm really looking forward to the Live Shows and I know I'm going to get very attached to the contestants. They all work really hard and they know that this is an amazing opportunity.

There are some absolutely fantastic singers this year. All the categories are very strong. I am hugely excited about working with them, and I feel very lucky to be on the show.

Craig Colton

Samantha Brookes

"The contestants have to withstand the TREMENDOUS PRESSURE of singing live each week."

X-CLUSIVE EXPERT TIP:

Stay hydrated! It is very hard to overstate the importance of drinking enough water. You should aim to drink two litres a day — it makes an enormous difference to how your voice can function.

Marcus Collins

X-CLUSIVE EXPERT TIP:

Appropriate breathing is an important part of caring for your voice. You need to make sure that you are not breathing too much! Your breathing should be appropriate to the vocal task. A good teacher can help you with this.

Kitty Brucknell

X-CLUSIVE EXPERT TIP:

If you are serious about progressing your career, get vocal training.

X-CLUSIVE EXPERT TIP:

Good posture has a huge impact on your voice. You need efficient posture to sing to your best ability. It's all about the relationship between your head, neck and back. It should be more relaxed than a military posture but not slouching forward. The body needs to work for the voice.

Terry Winstanley

Bradley Johnson

X-CLUSIVE EXPERT TIP:

If you have a sore throat, the best advice is to go and see the doctor and get a professional opinion. Your voice is your instrument, and you have to take care of it.

Holly Repton

X-CLUSIVE EXPERT TIP:

Stay away from singing anything very popular in your Audition unless you have a different take on it. You'll end up imitating the original instead of sounding like yourself.

Estrella

X-CLUSIVE EXPERT TIP:

You should feel comfortable with what you sing. It shouldn't feel strained — never push your voice to an extreme. If your speaking voice is husky or tired after you practise, it's a sign that you are working too hard or inefficiently.

CHOREOGRAPHY

To put on the best performance possible, it's important to think about the overall impression you're going to create onstage. The way that you move will play a big part in how the audience and the Judges see you.

Creative director Brian Burke and creative director and choreographer Elizabeth Honan have some useful advice to help you put on the best Audition you possibly can!

ELIZABETH & BRIAN
X FACTOR'S CHOREOGRAPHY X-PERTS

Elizabeth and Brian work on the Live Shows to put together the performances for the artists. They focus on the choreography and the visual look, which includes lighting, what appears on the screen behind each artist and the overall mood of the performance.

Heshima Thompson

What do you look for at Audition stage?

People who show that they have put a lot of work in. The best Auditionees are the ones who come across as friendly, warm and accessible, with a positive attitude. They wear their heart on their sleeve so you get their personality straight away. And of course, they have to have that special something

What makes a contestant stand out visually for you?

Someone with a really individual style – not your typical jeans and a T-shirt. It might be something that portrays their personality or their musical style. An interesting outfit shows that they have made an effort.

Wagner
Series 7

Goldie Cheung

"Goldie is incredible. WHAT A CHARACTER!"

How would you define 'star quality'?

It's a special ingredient that you can't create – you've either got it or you haven't. It's what gets people talking about you. You need to have a positive attitude, openness and talent, but you also need that extra something to be able to win *The X Factor*.

What puts you off an Auditionee?

You can just feel it if someone thinks that they are better than everyone else or doesn't want to learn. Auditionees need to be aware that they are surrounded by people who have worked in the business for many years. It would be stupid to go onstage thinking that they know better than everyone else.

What is the best way for an Auditionee to practise?

It's best to perform in front of a bunch of mates rather than family. Look them in the eyes and don't get silly. Even better, sing in front of strangers. They will give an unbiased opinion.

Sarah Watson

Diva Fever
Series 7

Indigo Rose

What do you find most exciting about your job?

The variety! You can create a really exciting spectacle onstage, which is great fun. But working on the lighting for a contestant who is simply standing still and singing a song can be just as important and exciting. It's all about the emotion that you can create.

How should an Auditionee choreograph moves for a song?

Listen to the song again and again and again. Keep dancing to it, listening to the words and thinking about what the song is saying. Then you can start piecing things together.

Francis Cardoso

You worked on the choreography at Bootcamp. Who do you think has the X factor this year?

Bootcamp is a crazy time! There are so many people there and we only get to work with them for a very short period of time, so we don't get to know them all personally. There were lots of people we really enjoyed working with, and the Girls category is very exciting – there's a lot of young talent there.

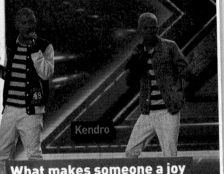

Kendro

What makes someone a joy to work with?

The best contestants are the ones who come in and can't wait to get started! It's all about enthusiasm. They might not be the most natural movers, but they are eager to practise again and again until they get it right. A negative attitude is definitely the hardest thing to work with!

Tara Burgin
197278

David Wilder

Jada Jax

"There is NOTHING LIKE THE BUZZ of creating something onstage."

X-CLUSIVE EXPERT TIP:

Practise really hard before you go in and make sure that you have fully gone through what you need to do.

Frankie Cocozza

X-CLUSIVE EXPERT TIP:

If you are too scared to make eye contact with the Judges, focus on a point in the distance. A simple technique to stop you being nervous is to imagine that the people in the audience are all members of your family.

X-CLUSIVE EXPERT TIP:

Confidence is good, but arrogance is bad.

Jesy Nelson

X-CLUSIVE EXPERT TIP:

Act confident! Walk onto the stage looking as if you belong there and should be a star. Hold your head up and your shoulders back, and have a good, confident walk.

Michael Lewis

X-CLUSIVE EXPERT TIP:

Don't look down at the ground and don't close your eyes when you're singing. Don't dart your eyes everywhere either — it makes you look nervous.

James Michael

X-CLUSIVE EXPERT TIP:

A bad attitude is really off-putting.

X-CLUSIVE EXPERT TIP:

Match your moves to the song. If you're a great dancer but the song doesn't ask for it, forget your moves. Just think about the song you are performing.

X-CLUSIVE EXPERT TIP:

Put together your own outfit and give it a lot of thought.

Goldie Cheung

X-CLUSIVE EXPERT TIP:

When you practise at home, stand in front of a full-length mirror. You need to be able to see what your body is doing when you're singing. Does your hand clench? Do you have any nervous tics? Watch yourself perform, because that's the only way you'll pick up on these things. They can be really off-putting, and you don't want the Judges to be distracted from your singing.

Boy v Girl

66296

X-CLUSIVE EXPERT TIP:

Keep pushing forward and take the knocks as well as the good times. If this really is your dream then approach everything with a positive attitude. Think 'Yes I can!'

X-CLUSIVE EXPERT TIP:

Deliver your song as if it is the last time you will ever sing it, and think about the meaning of every word you're singing.

THE BUILD UP

The weeks leading up to your Audition will be hugely exciting. This is going to be one of the biggest days of your life, and you want it to be perfect.

The key is in the amount of preparation you do. The best Auditionees are those who have done lots of preparation, so think carefully about how you are going to spend that time.

AS SOON AS POSSIBLE

Decide which songs you are going to prepare for your Audition. All Auditionees are asked to bring five tracks, including one acapella, make sure you know them inside out and back to front.
Plan out your schedule for the next few weeks. Allow yourself time for relaxation and fun as well as rehearsing. Creative artists need time away from their craft to recharge their batteries!

THE MONTH BEFORE

Book a place to stay if you need to be away from home for the night. Hotels and guest houses can get very busy around the time of *The X Factor* Auditions, so the earlier you book the better.

Start planning your image. If you are making your outfit, now's the time to start looking for fabric and inspiration!

Organise a date to perform a small gig in front of an audience. Think about this as a rehearsal for your Audition. Ask people to give you honest feedback - and be prepared to listen to what they say! Write down all the comments that you hear, and think about what you might need to work on before the big day.

Watch past Auditions and make some notes about which ones you liked best. What did you notice about the successful Auditionees? Can you pick up any hints or tips that might help you?

TWO WEEKS BEFORE

Check the route you will be taking to the venue. If you live nearby travel there and see how long it will take. If you live far away, use the internet to estimate how long your journey will take. Finalise the details of your outfit and put together any accessories you might want. Practise your chosen hairstyle and make-up. If you wish, get your hair cut and coloured. This will give it plenty of time to settle before the big day.

Think about what sort of questions the Judges are likely to ask you. Watching past Auditions will help you to guess what they might want to know. Prepare some answers in advance so that you're not taken by surprise. Finalise your outfit and try it with your hair styled and any make-up on. Stand in front of a full-length mirror and perform your Audition songs. This is your dress rehearsal, so aim to be word perfect!

THE NIGHT BEFORE

Check that your outfit is clean, ironed and ready for the morning.

Start to prepare your Audition bag. You could be waiting around for hours, so you should take anything you think you might need. This might include . . .

- ☐ Backing tracks
- ☐ Book or magazine
- ☐ Bottle of water
- ☐ Camera
- ☐ Comb
- ☐ Lunch
- ☐ Make-up
- ☐ Mobile phone charger
- ☐ Pen and paper
- ☐ Pocket mirror
- ☐ Snacks
- ☐ Song lyrics

Eat your fave meal with your fave people.

Set your alarm. This really isn't the right day to oversleep!

Charge your mobile phone overnight - you don't want to run out of battery.

Get an early night. You will need lots of energy tomorrow, so give yourself the best chance of feeling at your best in the morning.

THE BIG DAY

The day of the Audition dawns at last! Whether your nerves are shot to pieces or you're bounding out of bed to get to the venue, make sure that this is a day to remember.

The important thing is to stay as calm and in control as you possibly can. You are bound to be nervous, but that doesn't mean that you can't master your nerves! Performers have to do it all the time, so it's great practice for your career in music.

GET THE LOOK

Give yourself plenty of time to have an invigorating shower and get into your outfit for the day. If you have planned a complicated hairstyle, don't rush it. You need to leave the house looking your best.

TRIPLE CHECK

Yes, you checked your bag last night, but if you have forgotten anything, this is your last chance! Make sure that you have everything you need before you leave the house – use the checklist on page 33 to help you.

BREAKFAST

It's absolutely vital that you eat a good breakfast today. You could be facing many long hours of waiting around, and you need to keep feeling fit and energetic. Choose cereal, poached eggs on toast, yoghurt or fresh fruit. Drink plenty of water or juice.

FINAL REHEARSAL

Run through your songs one last time, but don't strain your voice. Think about the questions that the Judges might ask you and think about your answers.

SURPRISE!

Allow yourself plenty of time to cope with the unexpected. Whether you are travelling by train, bus, car or private jet, there's always a chance that something will go wrong. It's better to arrive for your Audition too early than too late.

SIGN IN

When you sign in and get your Audition number, make sure that you know where you are supposed to wait. Check out the locations of the toilets and the nearest food stand or shop. Then find a seat and get comfy – you might be in for quite a wait!

MAKE FRIENDS

Make the most of this fantastic opportunity and make some new friends. Think about it – the chances are that you're surrounded by people who share the same passion as you do. Smile at the people in the seats beside you. They may be feeling nervous, confused and excited all at the same time – just like you! Get chatting and you will soon forget about your nerves.

BE PATIENT

The Auditions can take a long time and there are a lot of people here to follow their dream, just like you. Let them have their moment in the spotlight and wait patiently – your chance to shine will come.

STAY FOCUSED

Don't get so caught up in the moment that you forget why you came! Take some time out to sit quietly and think about why you are here. Do vocal warm ups but don't over practice or make yourself more nervous.

GOOD LUCK!

When you step out onto the stage, you are also taking your first steps towards your chosen career. Use your nerves and excitement in a positive way, and pour your energy into your performance. This could be the first day of the rest of your life!

ELIMINATED!

So you have fought your way through Auditions, Bootcamp and Judges Houses, and you have made it into the Live Shows . . . only to be eliminated early on. What could you have done to stay in?

Check out these eliminated acts from the early weeks of last year's show. What do you think went wrong for them – and what can you learn from their experiences?

NICOLO FESTA

WEEK OF ELIMINATION: 1

Also in bottom three: Belle Amie and F.Y.D.
Eliminated by: Judges/Audience votes

Verdict: Nicolo was eliminated because the audience didn't respond to his quirky character.

Lesson: It is risky to rely too heavily on a quirky personality or an unusual look. If you stand out from the crowd, make sure that you have the vocals to back up your attitude!

JUDGES COMMENTS:

"I didn't like it." **Cheryl**

"You're a diva." **Louis**

"You are my big risk." **Dannii**

"I think you look better than you sound." **Simon**

JOHN ADELEYE

WEEK OF ELIMINATION: 3

JUDGES COMMENTS:

"You sang it so well." **Dannii**

"You always deliver." **Cheryl**

"You gave it everything." **Simon**

"You totally owned the stage." **Louis**

Also in bottom two: Treyc Cohen
Eliminated by: Judges/Audience votes

Verdict: John was eliminated because the audience hadn't got to know him as well as they had some of the other acts.

Lesson: Let the audience get to know you through your interviews and your performance. Open up during your song, and focus on your connection with the crowd. The most successful pop stars are skilled at bonding with their audience, so don't let shyness or embarrassment hold you back.

DIVA FEVER

WEEK OF ELIMINATION: 2

Also in bottom three: Belle Amie and Storm Lee
Eliminated by: Judges/Audience votes

Verdict: Diva Fever were eliminated because although they were lots of fun, they didn't have as much potential for improvement as Belle Amie.

Lesson: It is vital to show versatility, even as early as week two. At this early stage, dare to push your limits and show the audience and the Judges how much more you have to offer. It's great to show that you are having a good time, but make sure it's clear that you are working hard as well.

JUDGES COMMENTS:

"I like you guys." **Dannii**

"You made everybody smile." **Louis**

"You do just seem like you're having the time of your lives." **Cheryl**

"You are fun." **Simon**

BELLE AMIE
WEEK OF ELIMINATION: 4

Also in bottom two: Katie Waissel
Eliminated by: Judges/Audience votes

Verdict: Belle Amie were eliminated because their vocals were not as strong as Katie's.

Lesson: It's important to focus on your image, but not at the expense of your vocals. Week by week the Judges are looking for improvement in your singing techniques and abilities. Don't spend so much time on your look that you neglect your sound.

JUDGES COMMENTS:

"You're getting your act together – you look like a really good girl band." **Louis**

"I would like to see you do something that's not 'girl band does girl band' again." **Cheryl**

"The vocals were not on track – if you put as much effort into the vocals it would have come across." **Dannii**

"I loved the costumes . . . it was your best performance so far." **Simon**

F.Y.D.
WEEK OF ELIMINATION: 1

STORM LEE
WEEK OF ELIMINATION: 2

JUDGES COMMENTS:

"You sing very well." **Dannii**

"I would actually really like to see you just stand there and sing." **Cheryl**

"You're just all over the place." **Simon**

Also in bottom three: Diva Fever and Belle Amie
Eliminated by: Judges/Audience votes

Verdict: Storm was eliminated because his image and performance overwhelmed his vocals.

Lesson: It's great to be able to put on a show, but make sure that the audience doesn't suspect you of hiding behind your image. They want to be able to hear you sing, and so do the Judges. Let your true personality guide your performance.

JUDGES COMMENTS:

"When you can dance and perform, the singing will come." **Cheryl**

"I think you're probably better dancers than singers." **Louis**

"You've been great, guys." **Simon**

Also in bottom three: Katie Waissel and Nicolo Festa
Eliminated by: Judges/Audience votes

Verdict: F.Y.D. were eliminated because their dance moves were better than their vocals.

Lesson: The audience will notice if you cover up weak vocals with too much choreography. Especially in week one it is extremely important that your performance shows off your vocals. The audience knows that you will improve as the weeks go by, but they need to know where you are starting from.

X-CONTESTANTS WHO HAVE MADE IT BIG

If you receive a no at any stage, don't give up. Lots of people have been sent away and gone on to follow their dreams.

Just because you aren't ready now, doesn't mean you never will be. Check out these familiar faces – for them, giving up simply wasn't an option!

MAX GEORGE

Long before he was in **The Wanted**, Max decided to Audition for *The X Factor*. He was sixteen at the time, and he was overwhelmed to get yesses from all three Judges. At Bootcamp, however, everything started to go wrong. After a poor performance, Max was sent home.

Despite his disappointment, Max didn't give up on his dreams. He used the positive feedback from his Audition to give him the energy to keep trying. After he had done a few gigs, he returned to *The X Factor*, this time as part of a band. Although they made it through to the Live Shows, they had to leave because they had a manager, which was against the rules.

Max kept focusing on the positive things that came out of his experiences, and now his hard work and perseverance has paid off. He's part of one of the most exciting boy bands in the UK, and the future is looking fantastic!

ALEXANDRA BURKE

Even 2008 *X Factor* winner **Alexandra Burke** was rejected the first time she Auditioned for the show! She made it through to the Final seven in Louis' category in 2005, but she was not chosen for the Live Shows.

Although she was disappointed, Alexandra didn't let this knock-back crush her ambitions. She took professional singing lessons, dedicating herself to making her dreams come true.

When she Auditioned again three years later, Alexandra had developed in ability and confidence. Cheryl chose to put her through to the Live Shows, and her outstanding performances ensured her place in the Final, where she was crowned the winner.

Since winning *The X Factor*, Alexandra's rise to fame has been dazzling, with an array of awards, hit singles and bestselling albums to her name

SURVIVORS' TIPS

Ask what the Judges think you can do to improve – and follow their advice!

Think about how you can develop as a singer.

Try getting some singing lessons or setting up a live performance at a local venue.

Work on your whole performance.

Learn how to control your nerves and really work the audience – being an entertainer isn't *just* about having a great voice.

If you're a solo singer, consider getting some musical friends together and forming a group.

Persevere!

TOM PARKER

MOLLIE KING

Before she was in **The Saturdays**, Mollie was a member of a girl band called Fallen Angelz. They Auditioned for *The X Factor* in 2007, and impressed the Judges with their unique version of 'Girlfriend'. Unfortunately they weren't as successful at Bootcamp, and they failed to make it through to the next stage of the competition.

Although the rejection was a blow, Mollie decided to take it as a sign that she needed to move in a different direction. She left Fallen Angelz and Auditioned to become a member of a new girl band called The Saturdays.

Tom longed for a career in music, and he Auditioned for *The X Factor* when he was sixteen. He didn't make it past the Auditions and his confidence took a big knock. Music was still his passion, but some time passed before he found the self-belief to do a live gig at a small local venue.

The gig was a huge success, and it gave Tom the push he needed to perform regularly and develop his writing and singing skills. Tom is now a member of **The Wanted**, and he's there because he held on to his dream and never, ever gave up!

THE REST, AS THEY SAY, IS **HISTORY!**

X-CLUSIVE TIPS FOR THE TOP

Over the years, hundreds of thousands of people have Auditioned for *The X Factor*. Some of them have gone on to become international recording artists. Others fell at the first hurdle. If you want to succeed, you need to learn from all them!

It's important to know what you should do at your Audition, but it's just as vital to know what you *shouldn't* **do.**

CASE STUDY: CHER LLOYD

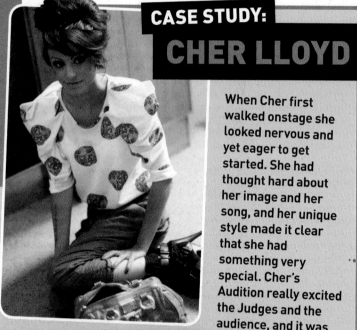

When Cher first walked onstage she looked nervous and yet eager to get started. She had thought hard about her image and her song, and her unique style made it clear that she had something very special. Cher's Audition really excited the Judges and the audience, and it was the start of her blossoming career.

CASE STUDY: DANYL JOHNSON

Simon Cowell thought that Danyl's Audition was the best he had ever seen. Danyl showed confidence, showmanship and style, and he brimmed with talent. He made lots of eye contact, his personality shone through and he listened carefully to what the Judges had to say. Danyl made it all the way through to the Live Shows.

• Match your moves to your song. If the lyrics are sad and still, don't leap around the stage!

• If you are in a band, make sure that you share the same attitudes towards the competition. It only takes one band member to give the whole group a bad reputation.

Lucie was shy and awkward at her Audition, but she focused on her dream and gave a beautiful performance. Even though she wasn't bursting with confidence, her quiet manner won the hearts of the audience. She went through to the Live Shows and developed in confidence and ability.

• Pick the right outfit. You can put the Judges and the audience off before you sing a note.

• Respect the fact that the Judges have years of experience and are giving you their time and attention.

• Be confident without being cocky. The Judges expect you to believe in yourself, but they don't expect you to tell them that you're better than Lady Gaga.

CASE STUDY: LUCIE JONES

CASE STUDY: ANGEL

Girl band Angel made a name for themselves for all the wrong reasons when one of them was rude to the Judges in Liverpool. She was not prepared to listen to criticism or to learn from it, and she embarrassed the other girls in the band with her attitude. They earned themselves a telling-off from Kelly Rowland, but no place at Bootcamp.

• Play to your strengths – if you have cool moves, don't keep them hidden away. This is your opportunity to show off!

• Be ready to sing more than one song. The Judges may ask you if you have prepared anything else.

• Only bring your friends and family along if you are sure that they won't upstage you and have you remembered for the wrong reason. Having your irate mum rushing onstage to defend you against criticism is not going to make you popular!

• Be prepared – if you forget the lyrics or get the timing wrong, you may have blown your big chance.

• Dare to be different. Using new words to an established song can really make the Judges sit up and take notice – as long as you do it well!

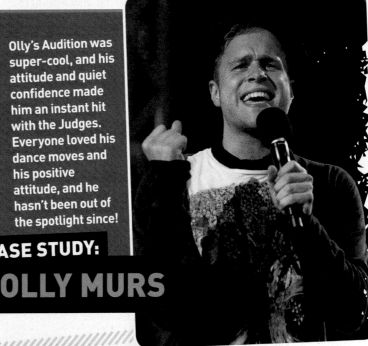

Olly's Audition was super-cool, and his attitude and quiet confidence made him an instant hit with the Judges. Everyone loved his dance moves and his positive attitude, and he hasn't been out of the spotlight since!

CASE STUDY: OLLY MURS

When George didn't get the response he wanted from the Judges, he became very rude. He insulted Tulisa and turned the audience against him. It took just a few short seconds to make himself look foolish on national TV. Needless to say, he didn't win a place at Bootcamp!

CASE STUDY: GEORGE GERASIMOU

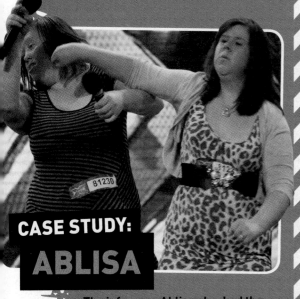

CASE STUDY: ABLISA

The infamous Ablisa shocked the nation when they turned on the Judges – and then on each other! They will be remembered for all the wrong reasons.

• If it's a no, thank the Judges and leave the stage with dignity. Arguing with their decision will just make you look childish.

• Make eye contact with the Judges.

• Remember your manners and don't be rude to the Judges. By Auditioning you are asking for their opinions, so keep your temper even if you don't like what you hear.

• Prepare your whole performance in advance and rehearse as much as you can. Organise a small gig if you're feeling daring!

THE AUDITIONS

The UK's biggest and boldest entertainment show came back with a bang in 2011, with three new Judges, two new *Xtra Factor* presenters and an exciting line up of twists and turns to the format.

The Judges trawled the cities of Great Britain in their quest to find the next singing superstars. People flocked to the Auditions, but there was a long journey ahead of the hopeful contestants who joined the queues.

Some people turned up on a whim, while others had been preparing for months or even years. Whatever their background, when they stepped onto the stage in front of the Judges they were each given the same chance.

Contestants Auditioned in four categories – Boys (16–24 years), Girls (16–24 years), Groups and Over-25s. Each individual or group faced Gary, Kelly, Tulisa and Louis, trying to prove that they had the magical ingredients that make a superstar.

Every time a new act opened their mouth to sing, the audience and the Judges waited with breathless excitement. Sometimes the sound was spectacular and sometimes it was disappointing, but the tension was always immense. An act had to receive at least three 'yesses' to make it through to Bootcamp, and emotions were running high!

Flick through the following pages and remind yourself of the highs and lows of the Auditions. Enjoy the surprises and dramas all over again, and decide if you think the Judges put the right people through!

> "There is no reason why the UK X Factor winner can't make a mark all over the world."
>
> *Kelly*

> "This is all about finding someone who genuinely want. a career in the music industry and is willing to work for that."
>
> *Louis*

Over 1.5 million requests for tickets!

"Each city brought a different vibe to the table."
Tulisa

"Overall, there have been about ten acts which have really stood out for me."
Gary

Biggest surprise of the Auditions?

Which city had the best talent?

88,600 people watched the Auditions!

GLASGOW
VENUE: Glasgow SECC
DATES: 6th June

MANCHESTER
VENUE: Manchester Event City
DATES: 12th, 13th &14th June

LIVERPOOL
VENUE: Liverpool Echo Arena
DATES: 13th & 14th July

Most memorable Audition?

First time for Auditions through Facebook and YouTube

People queued for over 6 hours to watch the Auditions!

BIRMINGHAM
VENUE: Birmingham LG Arena
DATES: 1st & 2nd June

Funniest Audition moment?

CARDIFF
VENUE: Cardiff CIA
DATES: 29th June

LONDON
VENUE: London O2 Arena
DATES: 6th, 7th & 8th July

HELLO LONDON

The Auditions reached the capital city, and the Judges couldn't wait to start their search for a star.

Crowds flocked to The O2 and went wild with excitement as the next generation of Judges entered the arena. The new panel was ready for action and all the Auditionees were hoping to make a fantastic impression. Destiny, dreams and passions hung in the air – *The X Factor* 2011 had begun!

FAMOUS LONDON MUSICIANS

LILY ALLEN   ELTON JOHN

AMY WINEHOUSE   WHAM   BLUR

ROLLING STONES   COLDPLAY

PLAN B   N-DUBZ   TINIE TEMPAH

DAVID BOWIE   THE WHO

DIZZEE RASCAL

Ellen Chetcuti
Age: 47   Song: 'What A Feeling'

Ellen's energetic performance left the audience and Judges speechless

GARY: NO   KELLY: NO
TULISA: NO   LOUIS: NO

RESULT: Ellen went home disappointed.

"I like you LADIES!"

SOSO Status
Age: 18   Song: 'Rockstar'

Denise, Brenda, Shannan and Grace were an instant hit with the audience.

GARY: YES   KELLY: YES   TULISA: YES   LOUIS: YES

RESULT: The girls were squealing with excitement as they came off the stage!

Dolled Up

"You were AMAZING!"

Roxy Yarnold
Age: 19   Song: 'Georgia'

Roxy blew everyone away with her amazing vocals. Gary compared her voice to brown sugar!

**GARY: YES   KELLY: YES
TULISA: YES   LOUIS: YES**

RESULT: Roxy headed for Bootcamp with four yesses under her belt!

Chi Chi

Hiba Elchikhe

Candice Barron

David Wilder

Louis Costa

"That was INCREDIBLE."

Heshima Thompson
Age: 24   Song: 'OMG'

Heshima's smooth voice and even smoother moves had the crowd on their feet and cheering.

**GARY: YES   KELLY: YES
TULISA: YES   LOUIS: YES**

RESULT: The Judges were impressed and Heshima was destined for Bootcamp.

"I felt alot of AGGRESSION from you."

George Gerasimou
Age: 19   Song: 'Give Me Everything'

George's first Audition in 2009 went badly, so he came back to show that he had matured and controlled his temper. However, after a disappointing Audition it seemed that his attitude still needed some work.

**GARY: NO
KELLY: NO
TULISA: NO
LOUIS: NO**

RESULT: The Judges felt that George still had some growing up to do.

HELLO LONDON

Lascel Wood

The Dollys

"I would like to see you in A GROUP."

Derry Mensah
Age: 20 **Song:** 'Can U Help Me'

Derry has two dreams – becoming a huge superstar and marrying Kelly Rowland! He sang his Audition without music, and won rapturous applause from the crowd. But did Kelly like it?

GARY: YES **KELLY: YES**
TULISA: YES **LOUIS: YES**

RESULT: The Judges really enjoyed Derry's Audition and he was soon on his way to Bootcamp with four yesses – and a kiss from his idol!

"You're a real SOUL MAN."

Jamie Bruce
Age: 32 **Song:** 'Signed, Sealed, Delivered I'm Yours'

Bouncer Jamie has wanted to be a singer since he was a child. His fantastic Audition had the audience dancing in the aisles!

KELLY: YES **TULISA: YES**
LOUIS: YES

RESULT: Jamie left with an invitation to Bootcamp.

Francis Cardoso

Tara Burgin

Glow

Michael Lewis
Age: 27 **Song:** 'Look At Me'

After his disastrous audition last year, Michael returned promising a new attitude and a new style.

GARY: NO **KELLY: NO**
TULISA: NO **LOUIS: NO**

RESULT: Michael didn't like the reaction he got from the Judges and the audience, and Gary had to get up onstage before he would agree to leave!

"It was just all A BIT WEIRD."

Ann Tunstall

Ben Morrell

Ginger Tops

Jesy Nelson

Samantha Hallam

Age: 37 **Song:** 'Sex On Fire'

Samantha's Audition was interrupted when her boyfriend came out on stage to propose. She said yes – and so did the Judges!

GARY: YES **KELLY:** YES
TULISA: YES **LOUIS:** YES

RESULT: It was an unforgettable day for Samantha!

"I think you've got an AWFUL LOT to give."

Jo Beetlestone

Age: 24 **Song:** 'One And Only'

Jo made it to Bootcamp last year, but her lack of confidence let her down. This time she showed a lot more self-belief and the audience loved her performance!

GARY: YES **KELLY:** YES
TULISA: YES **LOUIS:** YES

RESULT: Jo got a second chance to prove herself at Bootcamp.

"You really CAN'T SING."

JTE

Age: 18 & 26 **Song:** 'Freak Me'

Rob and William turned up for the Auditions with big dreams and high hopes. They put on an entertaining show and the audience loved them.

GARY: NO **KELLY:** NO **TULISA:** NO **LOUIS:** NO

RESULT: The Judges thought they were great fun but the talent wasn't there.

"I didn't really UNDERSTAND what you were saying."

Sergei Muraujai

Age: 26 **Song:** 'Russian Rapper'

The self-titled Russian Rapper has been rapping since he was sixteen. He came to the Auditions to pursue his dream of rap stardom, and his performance electrified the arena.

GARY: NO **KELLY:** NO
TULISA: NO **LOUIS:** YES

RESULT: People in the crowd were dancing, but the Judges were not as enthusiastic!

HELLO MANCHESTER

Gary's appearance prompted the biggest turnout in Manchester's *X Factor* history. Everyone wanted to impress him and the crowds were chanting his name.

With Take That performing live in Manchester, Gary was very busy, but he was also keen to find a star. The contestants were excited, the Judges were hopeful and the crowds were hysterical – time to start the Auditions!

FAMOUS **MANCHESTER** MUSICIANS

OASIS   **THE STONE ROSES**   HAPPY MONDAYS

THE CHARLATANS   TAKE THAT

THE VERVE   JAY KAY   **THE BEE GEES**   DAVID GRAY

MORRISSEY   THE SMITHS

"I'm actually in SHOCK."

Dalton

Jane Belfield
Age: 55 **Song:** Own rap 'Things We Do'

Jane really took the Judges by surprise with her rap!

GARY: **NO**   KELLY: **NO**
TULISA: **NO**   LOUIS: **YES**

RESULT: The Judges appreciated Jane's hardwork, but felt that there wasn't a market for her.

Celeste

"That was what you call ENTERTAINMENT"

Becky Shaw

Ashley Crowe

Ron Davis
Age: 43 **Song:** 'Ain't Too Proud To Beg'

Texas-born Ron brought the cool factor to the stage!

GARY: **YES**   KELLY: **YES**
TULISA: **YES**   LOUIS: **YES**

RESULT: Ron charmed the Judges and made it through to Bootcamp.

Elliot Nichol

"It's just not going TO WORK."

"I really HAD FUN watching you guys."

Kendro
Age: 18-23 **Song:** 'Born This Way'

Hoping for worldwide success, the boys came out onstage and delivered a fun-filled performance.

GARY: **NO**   KELLY: **YES**   TULISA: **YES**   LOUIS: **YES**

RESULT: Kendro had great enthusiasm but not all the Judges were impressed with their vocals.

Honey Shazaad

Callum Scanlon
Age: 17 **Song:** 'Pass Out'

Callum, also known as K-Zo, loves to rap and had the audience clapping along at his Audition.

GARY: **NO**   KELLY: **NO**
TULISA: **NO**   LOUIS: **NO**

RESULT: The Judges didn't think that rapping was Callum's future.

HELLO MANCHESTER

Chess Leigh

Regan-Pia-Carra Pyce

Intrigue

"I don't think YOU'RE READY."

Kibo Hunt
Age: 17 Song: 'Nobody's Perfect'

Inspired by Rihanna, Kibo turned up for her audition believing that she was unlike any other artist in the world.

GARY: NO   KELLY: NO
TULISA: NO LOUIS: NO

RESULT: The Judges thought that Kibo looked gorgeous, but her voice needed work.

Beverley Saurin

"You started to sing and the ROOM LIT UP."

Basil Simoneko
Age: 46 Song: 'The House Of The Rising Sun'

Basil had hidden his true character behind a mask, but the Judges were determined to get to know the real man.

GARY: YES   KELLY: YES
TULISA: YES LOUIS: YES

RESULT: Despite a shaky start, Basil headed off to Bootcamp!

Rachel Arnison

"Yes please – all the way TO THE LEFT."

Andy Brooks
Age: 17 Song: 'To The Left'

Could beauty student Andy prove Gary's theory that the north-west has the best talent in the country?

GARY: NO KELLY: NO TULISA: NO LOUIS: NO

RESULT: Andy failed to excite the Judges.

Laura Ranmell

2 Brothers
Age: 18 Song: 'It's Tricky'

The boys wanted to be as big as Run DMC and had plenty of confidence. The Judges thought they were great characters!

GARY: NO   KELLY: NO
TULISA: NO LOUIS: NO

RESULT: The performance wasn't good enough to win a place at Bootcamp.

Zavia Hill

"You are so CHARMING."

Tyla Durden

Kid City

Christine Rodgerson
Age: 50 Song: 'It's Raining Men'

Christine threw herself into her performance!

GARY: NO KELLY: NO TULISA: NO LOUIS: NO

RESULT: The Judges sent Christine home without an invitation to Bootcamp.

Cookie

Paper Roses

"It is a SINGING COMPETITION – that's the problem."

Carl Stephenson
Age: 21 Song: 'Beautiful People'

Carl just wanted to dance!

**GARY: NO   KELLY: NO
TULISA: NO   LOUIS: NO**

RESULT: Carl had great energy but his singing let him down.

"Thanks for coming along, BUT IT'S A NO."

Section 2
Age: 34 & 38 Song: 'Me And My Shadow'

Double act Michael and Bruce had great fun onstage, but their singing didn't excite the Judges.

GARY: NO KELLY: NO TULISA: NO LOUIS: NO

RESULT: Section 2's dream of winning *The X Factor* was over.

"You two would be GREAT IN COMEDY."

Lemuel Knights
Age: 16 Song: 'Georgia'

Lemuel waited for years to appear on the show, and his audition blew the Judges away!

**GARY: YES   KELLY: YES
TULISA: YES   LOUIS: YES**

RESULT: The Judges were really excited when they heard Lemuel sing.

"I thought your voice was ABSOLUTELY TERRIFIC."

HELLO CARDIFF

Wales has produced some of the best singers in the music industry, so the Judges felt really excited when they arrived in Cardiff!

As the Welsh audiences queued and the Auditionees waited nervously backstage, the Judges got ready to see what Cardiff had to offer. Would the winner of *The X Factor* 2011 make their first appearance today?

FAMOUS SOUTH WALES MUSICIANS

TOM JONES · BONNIE TYLER · STEREOPHONICS

FEEDER · MANIC STREET PREACHERS

SHIRLEY BASSEY · CHARLOTTE CHURCH

SHAKIN' STEVENS · SUPER FURRY ANIMALS

CERYS MATTHEWS

Limitless

Another Planet

"You came out on that stage HOWLING!"

"The good news is you've STOPPED SINGING"

Danielle Phillips Green

Alan House

Ceri Hoey
Age: 42 Song: 'Wuthering Heights'

Ceri's high-pitched vocal had the Judges wide eyed with astonishment.

GARY: **NO**   KELLY: **NO**
TULISA: **NO**   LOUIS: **NO**

RESULT: Ceri didn't get invited to Bootcamp.

Mitchell Webb
Age: 28 Song: 'Angel'

Bar worker Mitchell turned up for his Audition hoping for a place at Bootcamp. He believed that with his looks and style, he could bring something special to the show.

GARY: **NO** KELLY: **NO** TULISA: **NO** LOUIS: **NO**

RESULT: Mitchell's performance didn't convince the Judges that he had what it takes!

Chelsea Redfern

O'Brien Hesson

"I'm not saying no – I'm saying NEVER!"

"It was just MADNESS!"

Natasha Paton Ali
Age: 23 Song: 'Everytime We Touch'

Natasha had singing lessons to prepare for her Audition, but Gary thought she should ask for a refund.

GARY: **NO**   KELLY: **NO**
TULISA: **NO**   LOUIS: **NO**

RESULT: The Judges didn't know where to look!

Samantha Scanlon

Plop
Age: 25 Song: 'Ballroom Blitz'

Plop walked confidently onstage, although he was feeling nervous. He brought some fabulous friends along with him for moral support..

GARY: **NO**   KELLY: **NO**
TULISA: **YES**   LOUIS: **YES**

RESULT: The Judges found Plop fascinating, but he didn't sway them all.

Tamarebi Itombia

Sara Chan

"Everything was **WRONG.**"

Anthony Chisman

27726

Dafydd Morgan
Age: 41 Song: **'Bat Out Of Hell'**

Dafydd took some time to start singing!

GARY: NO   **KELLY: NO**
TULISA: NO   **LOUIS: NO**

RESULT: Dafydd's electrifying performance didn't persuade the Judges to send him to Bootcamp.

Jade Johnson

Alberto Diniz

108006

"Vocally it just wasn't **UP TO SCRATCH.**"

Catching Fire

117205

Joanna Robinson
Age: 48 Song: **'Here You Come Again'**

Hoping to be the UK's version of Nicole Scherzinger, Joanna walked onstage with confidence and gave Louis a scarf that she had knitted herself.

GARY: NO **KELLY: NO** **TULISA: NO** **LOUIS: YES**

RESULT: Joanna had fun, but she didn't make it through to Bootcamp.

Dane Loyd

NYD
Age: 50 & 49 Song: **'Thinking Of Me'**

This husband and wife team love singing together and have been married for twenty-five years. They were looking forward to sharing their music with the audience.

GARY: NO **KELLY: NO** **TULISA: NO** **LOUIS: NO**

RESULT: Olly was delighted that someone chose to sing his song, but the Judges said no.

Laura Anderson

"I think there's **SOMETHING GOOD HERE.**"

Brooklyn Age: **21, 22 & 24** Song: **'Forget You' / 'In My Head'**

These four mates had rehearsed in their bedrooms, and came along to their Audition determined to win.

GARY: **YES** KELLY: **NO** TULISA: **NO** LOUIS: **YES**

RESULT: The band made it through to Bootcamp, but they had a lot of hard work ahead of them.

Kathryn Birmingham

Holly Evans

Justin Johnson

Sean Scannell

"You've got a **LOT OF POTENTIAL.**"

John Adams

Age: **23** Song: **'Cannonball'**

After a string of unsuccessful Auditionees, the Judges were delighted by John's emotional vocal.

GARY: **YES** KELLY: **YES**
TULISA: **YES** LOUIS: **YES**

RESULT: John had the Cardiff crowds on their feet!

Krystal Buckley

HELLO GLASGOW

The X Factor headed north of the border, and the Judges prepared to seek out some Scottish talent!

The Auditions moved on to Glasgow, and thousands turned up to prove to the Judges that Scotland has the X factor. With them came an army of friends and relations to support them as they stepped onto the stage . . . and to comfort them if things went wrong.

FAMOUS GLASGOW MUSICIANS

THE FRATELLIS **TRAVIS** EDDI READER

FRANZ FERDINAND LULU **MARK KNOPFLER**

PRIMAL SCREAM **SIMPLE MINDS** DONOVAN

JIMMY SOMERVILLE BELLE & SEBASTIAN

DEACON BLUE DEL AMITRI

Lynn Harkness

Viva Glam

Raheem Tahir

Jim Devine

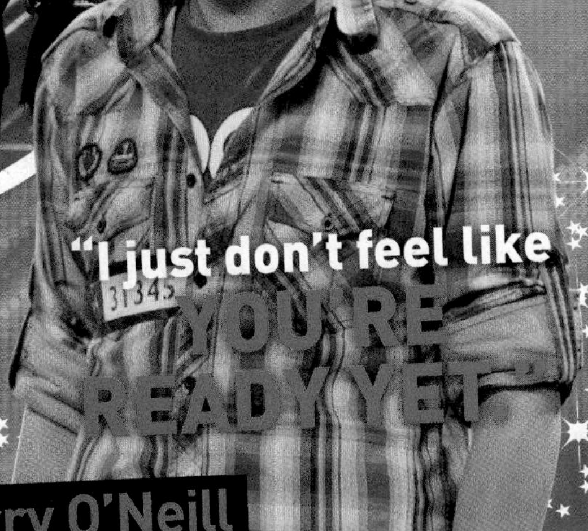

"I just don't feel like **YOU'RE READY YET**"

Harry O'Neill
Age: 17 **Song:** 'Rolling in the Deep'

Harry had a bad attack of stage fright and broke down halfway through his song.

GARY: NO TULISA: NO KELLY: NO LOUIS: NO

RESULT: Harry's nerves let him down, and the Judges advised him to get more experience.

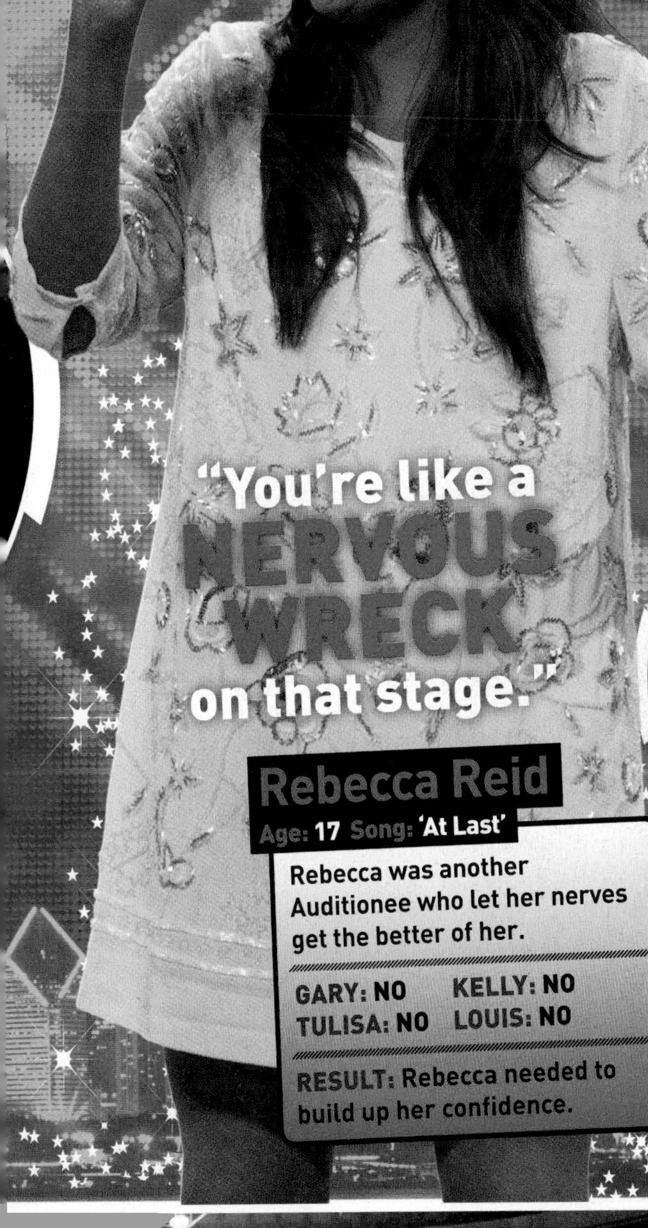

"You're like a **NERVOUS WRECK** on that stage."

Rebecca Reid
Age: 17 **Song:** 'At Last'

Rebecca was another Auditionee who let her nerves get the better of her.

**GARY: NO KELLY: NO
TULISA: NO LOUIS: NO**

RESULT: Rebecca needed to build up her confidence.

Arlene Johnson

Lee Connelly

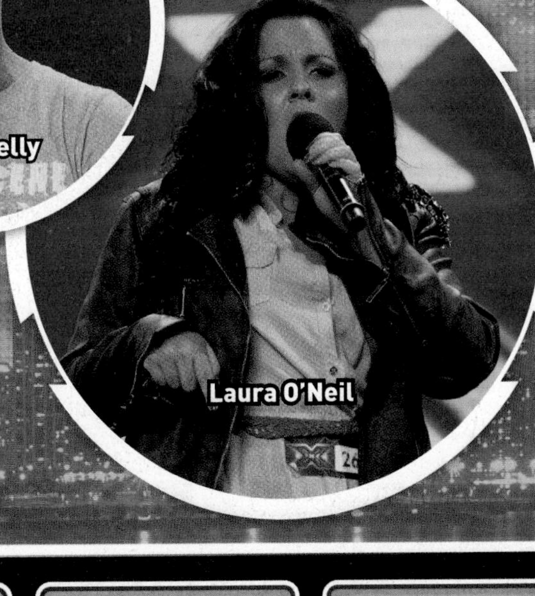

Laura O'Neil

HELLO GLASGOW

Aaron Deery

After the Rayn

Patricia Williams

Sarah Grant

"Find who your are as AN ARTIST."

Johnny McManus
Age: 20 Song: 'Do It Like a Dude'

Law student Johnny dreams of pop stardom, and he came to the Auditions hoping that this was his big chance. His performance took everyone by surprise!

GARY: YES   KELLY: NO
TULISA: YES LOUIS: YES

RESULT: The Judges were intrigued to see how Johnny would develop at Bootcamp.

Perrie Edwards
Age: 17 Song: 'Ave Maria' / 'You Oughta Know'

Perrie's vocals had the Judges squabbling! Could a second song prove that she had star quality?

GARY: YES   KELLY: YES
TULISA: YES   LOUIS: YES

RESULT: Perrie left the stage with four yesses!

"You came in here BLOWING this roof off!"

Alex Tonkindon

Rio Abernethy

Lillian C Nwae-ye

Beverly Birtles

Jim McElvar

"That was **VERY UNIQUE.**"

Broman5e Age: **17-18** Song: 'Black and Gold'

These five school friends teamed up to form a group, but it was lacking the magic ingredient that the Judges were looking for.

GARY: **NO** KELLY: **NO** TULISA: **NO** LOUIS: **NO**

RESULT: The boys had the look but they didn't have the voices to match.

Lexington

Kayleigh Waterfall

"It was **BRILLIANT.**"

Michelle Barrett

Age: **31** Song: 'All The Man That I Need'

Michelle plucked up the courage to Audition and pursue her lifelong dream.

GARY: **YES** KELLY: **YES** TULISA: **YES** LOUIS: **YES**

RESULT: Michelle's beautiful voice was a big hit with the audience and moved Tulisa to tears.

Rick Thurlow

Nicole Simpson

Alana Cope

HELLO LIVERPOOL

Liverpool went wild when *The X Factor* wagons rolled into town!

The Judges visited Liverpool for the first time this year, and thousands of the city's would-be stars queued up for the chance to appear on *The X Factor*. It's the home of the biggest group of all time, The Beatles, so the groups Auditioning had a big challenge on their hands. These Judges would be difficult to impress!

FAMOUS LIVERPOOL MUSICIANS

THE BEATLES   TEARDROP EXPLODES
THE ZUTONS   ATOMIC KITTEN   CILLA BLACK
ECHO & THE BUNNYMEN   FRANKIE GOES TO HOLLYWOOD   GERRY & THE PACEMAKERS
THE LIGHTNING SEEDS   GEORGE MELLY
THE MERSEYBEATS

"What a RACKET!"

Michael Schumacher
Age: 20   Song: 'Sweet Child o' Mine'

Guns 'N' Roses fan Michael wanted to inject some Vitamin Rock into *The X Factor*, but the Judges were not convinced!

GARY: NO   KELLY: NO   TULISA: NO   LOUIS: NO

RESULT: Louis liked the jumping around, but Michael's singing failed to impress.

Ciara Titchener

The Huhas

"I'm afraid your YOUR VOICE isn't up to scratch."

Ben Dillan
Age: 22   Song: 'Angels'

Ben visualised every moment of his Audition, and he had the crowd waving their arms in the air just as he had planned. However, the Judges' reaction took him by surprise . . .

GARY: NO   KELLY: NO   TULISA: NO   LOUIS: NO

RESULT: Ben went home without the good news he had hoped for.

Leigh Elson

Nathalie Makoma

"FANTASTIC!"

Gemma McDowell
Age: 18   Song: 'Somebody Else's Guy'

Gemma came along with actor Ricky Tomlinson to support her, and she totally wowed the crowd with her huge voice.

GARY: YES   KELLY: YES
TULISA: YES   LOUIS: YES

RESULT: Ricky Tomlinson believes that Gemma has the X factor, and the Judges agreed!

Sophie Bond

Joseph Castle
Age: 24   Song: 'Let There Be Love'

Joseph's sultry vocals sent Kelly all of a flutter!

GARY: YES   KELLY: YES
TULISA: YES   LOUIS: YES

RESULT: Joseph was destined for Bootcamp.

"It's going to be a YES!"

HELLO LIVERPOOL

Sunny Daye

"Sounded GORGEOUS."

Luigiano
Age: 18 **Song:** 'Ain't No Sunshine'

Luigiano was a Finalist in the Dutch *X Factor*, but he wanted to try his luck in the UK. His soulful voice captured the hearts of the audience and the Judges.

GARY: **YES**	KELLY: **YES**
TULISA: **YES**	LOUIS: **YES**

RESULT: Luigiano's passion shone through and he got a standing ovation!

"I'M FRUSTRATED with the bands."

Poetic Justice
Age: 25-27 **Song:** 'Rolling in the Deep'

The Judges were horrified by Poetic Justice's singing.

GARY: **NO**	KELLY: **NO**	TULISA: **NO**	LOUIS: **NO**

RESULT: The Judges cheered themselves up by thinking that things could only get better.

Shante Ashmeade

Christian Grigore

"You really have the element OF SURPRISE!"

Roger Boyd **Age:** 32
Song: 'I'd Do Anything for Love (But I Won't Do That)'

Roger was inspired to Audition by Susan Boyle. He was determined to show the Judges that he had something special, and the audience was soon dancing in the aisles!

GARY: **YES**	KELLY: **YES**	TULISA: **YES**	LOUIS: **YES**

RESULT: Roger was a massive hit with the audience and the Judges!

Tru Colorz

Kirsty Murphy

Sandra Bayad

"The singing was **TRULY HORRIBLE.**"

"It was a very **INTERESTING VERSION.**"

Mark Byron

Age: 21   **Song:** 'Only Girl (In The World)'

Mark wanted to show that Liverpool had the X factor . . . but perhaps he wasn't the one to prove it!

GARY: **NO**	KELLY: **NO**
TULISA: **NO**	LOUIS: **NO**

RESULT: The Judges were disappointed by Mark's vocals.

Deep Dhillion

Age: 52   **Song:** 'Back For Good'

The Judges liked Deep and his moves, but his voice wasn't strong enough to satisfy them.

GARY: **NO**	KELLY: **NO**
TULISA: **NO**	LOUIS: **YES**

RESULT: Deep didn't make it to Bootcamp.

Margaret Garner

Minx

Richard Moore

Angel

Age: 18-23   **Song:** 'Whip My Hair'

The girls in the band had plenty of energy, but things turned sour when the Judges criticised their singing.

GARY: **NO**   KELLY: **NO**   TULISA: **NO**   LOUIS: **NO**

RESULT: Angel's singing voices were not good enough – and neither was their attitude!

"An absolute massive **MASSIVE NO.**"

"I thought the vocals were **REALLY WEAK.**"

Danny Dwyer

Age: 18   **Song:** 'Pass Out'

N-Dubz fan Danny came along to the Auditions hoping to change his life.

GARY: **NO**	KELLY: **NO**
TULISA: **NO**	LOUIS: **NO**

RESULT: The Judges had to send Danny away disappointed.

HELLO BIRMINGHAM

The Judges were travelling the length and breadth of the country in the search for a superstar, and the Auditions moved on to Birmingham. Hordes of people turned up to welcome the Judges to their city. The arena was packed and dreams of fame and fortune filled the hearts of the Auditionees!

FAMOUS **BIRMINGHAM** MUSICIANS

BLACK SABBATH OCEAN CLOUR SCENE

OZZY OSBOURNE JAMELIA

THE STREETS TOYAH WILLCOX DURAN DURAN

John Hartley

"You could be PRETTY GOOD!"

Lillie Laverick

"This soul just comes BURSTING OUT of you."

Faye Horn
Age: 19 Song: 'She Said'

Faye started singing at thirteen, and she is passionate about performing. Her Audition was mesmerising and she enjoyed every minute.

GARY: YES KELLY: YES TULISA: YES LOUIS: YES

RESULT: The Judges applauded and the audience gave Faye a standing ovation!

Sarah-Louise Wills
Age: 20 Song: 'One Night Only'

Sarah's ditsy personality concealed a big, beautiful voice.

GARY: YES KELLY: YES TULISA: YES LOUIS: YES

RESULT: The Judges agreed that Sarah had the likeability factor, and just needed some training and confidence boosting.

"You have a lot of STAR QUALITY"

David Largie

Eugene McCarthy

"You're everything that we're not LOOKING FOR"

Ashford Campbell
Age: 19 Song: 'Senorita'

Student Ashford came to the Auditions ready to show the Judges his swagger! His vocals slipped in places, but he showed that he had bags of potential.

GARY: YES KELLY: YES TULISA: YES LOUIS: YES

RESULT: The Judges loved Ashford's super-cool style!

Randy Roxx
Age: 45 Song: 'Starman'

Randy's passion in life is to entertain people, but his Audition didn't get the audience excited enough.

GARY: NO KELLY: NO TULISA: NO LOUIS: NO

RESULT: Randy enjoyed his time onstage, but he didn't make it to Bootcamp.

HELLO BIRMINGHAM

Ian McKenzie

"The look's a LITTLE BIT CHEAP"

Sassy
Age: 17-20 Song: Own song 'Precious'

The Sassy girls weren't happy with their performance – and neither were the Judges.

GARY: **NO** KELLY: **NO** TULISA: **NO** LOUIS: **NO**

RESULT: The girls needed to work on their image and their sound.

Sophia Port

"Was it a DREAM?"

Bharat Battina
Age: 24 Song: 'C'mon (Catch em' by Surprise)'

Bharat's dance moves reminded Gary of Riverdance, but his voice didn't quite match up!

GARY: **NO**   KELLY: **NO**
TULISA: **NO**   LOUIS: **NO**

RESULT: The Judges sent Bharat home disappointed.

Marie Neil

Daz Stokes

Ray Harding

Kurtis Ray-White

"YOU'RE NEVER EVER going to go to Bootcamp, ever"

"I think it would be far TOO MUCH WORK to get you ready for this year – and next year."

Wendy Davis
Age: 30 Song: 'Wuthering Heights'

Wendy loves Britney Spears, and she turned up for the Auditions hoping to become as famous as her idol.

GARY: **NO**   KELLY: **NO**   TULISA: **NO**   LOUIS: **NO**

RESULT: When Gary covered his ears, it was obvious things weren't going to end well for Wendy . . .

Graham Bennett
Age: 52 Song: 'She Bangs'

Muscle-man Graham fantasised about having the glamorous life of a pop star, so he decided to move from karaoke to *The X Factor*.

GARY: **NO**   KELLY: **NO**
TULISA: **NO**   LOUIS: **NO**

RESULT: Graham's vocal skills were not good enough to please the Judges.

"I LOVED YOUR ABS a little bit more than I loved your voice."

"There's a LOT OF WORK –that needs to be done."

Tress

Age: 20-21 **Song:** 'Bust Your Windows'

Kelly taught this girl band a few singing techniques!

GARY: YES KELLY: YES TULISA: YES LOUIS: YES

RESULT: Tress had a lot of potential and were prepared to work hard to improve.

Perry Devonish

Age: 29 **Song:** 'I Have Nothing'

Perry impressed Kelly with his six pack, but sadly not with his singing!

GARY: NO KELLY: NO TULISA: NO LOUIS: NO

RESULT: Perry proved that it takes more than good looks to make star quality.

V-Box

Jem Fontanet

Penny Diamond

Jae Alexander

Demetrizia Cabatinga

Ana Emila Silva

Age: 23 **Song:** 'Rockstar 101'

Anamelia turned up for her Audition with plenty of attitude!

GARY: NO   KELLY: NO
TULISA: NO   LOUIS: NO

RESULT: The Judges felt that Anamelia needed to learn the difference between arrogance and confidence.

"You stepped over THE LINE"

Chelsea Sianga

BOOTCAMP

After the excitement and drama of the Auditions, 186 acts made their way to Bootcamp. Their time would be divided between Wembley Arena and a luxury hotel on the outskirts of London. Their biggest challenge yet was about to begin.

The first surprise of the week came when *The X Factor* coaches carried the excited contestants to a magnificent hotel. It would be their home for the next few days, but this was only the first of many surprises that the Judges had in store.

When the contestants reached their rooms, they found invitations to a Bootcamp Welcome Party on their beds. There was just one rule – they had to dress to impress!

The party was soon underway, complete with an *X Factor Ice Bar*, a chocolate fountain and hot tubs. But while the contestants enjoyed themselves, the Judges were having their own private get-together to decide the contestants' fate.

BOOTCAMP DAY ONE

THROUGH TO BOOTCAMP

GIRLS:	73
BOYS:	46
OVER 25s:	48
GROUPS:	18

The acts were relaxing in the sunshine when the Judges arrived in four executive cars. They had some shocking news to deliver. They had watched all the Auditions again, and decided that not everyone was talented enough to go any further in the competition. Some people would be going home right now!

The acts were divided into smaller groups to learn their fate. Most heard good news, but thirty-five disappointed contestants had to pack their bags. They would leave Bootcamp without singing a note.

The remaining contestants were set their first Bootcamp Challenge. After being split into teams, they were given one of six songs. They had three hours to practise together, and then they had to perform in front of the Judges at Wembley Arena. The pressure was on!

BOOTCAMP WELCOME PARTY

151 STILL STANDING

BOOTCAMP CHALLENGE 1 SONG LIST

'PRICE TAG'
by Jessie J

'FIREWORK'
by Katy Perry

'BREAKEVEN'
by The Script

'BORN THIS WAY'
by Lady Gaga

'FORGET YOU'
by Cee-Lo Green

'YOU'VE GOT THE LOVE'
by Florence And The Machine

BOOTCAMP BUZZ

Marlon McKenzie from The Risk made it to Dannii's house last year, but she didn't take him further in the competition.

BOOTCAMP
DAY TWO

The teams had all performed the day before, and after an anxious wait they were called back to Wembley Arena. The Judges were ready to tell them who would be going through to the next round – and who would be going home. It was a nerve-wracking time for all the acts, and emotions were running high.

After the Judges had given their verdicts, they had a problem to solve. They weren't happy with the small number of groups in the competition, but they had a daring idea. With their combined experience, could they put together some brand-new groups from the contestants they had rejected earlier?

Meanwhile, the successful contestants were back on the stage – choreographer Beth Honan had them working hard on a big dance routine. There's no time to rest at Bootcamp!

61 STILL STANDING

(((BOOTCAMP))) | JUDGES' HOUSES | THE FINAL 16 | LIVE SHOW SCRAPBOOK | LOOKING BACK

BOOTCAMP
DAY THREE

The contestants spent the day practising for their big moment which would take place the next day. They worked with vocal coaches and tried out their new dance moves with Beth. They even had the chance to find out how they looked through a lens, thanks to photographer Nicky Johnston.

The people who had been formed into new bands had the biggest challenge of all. In just twenty-four hours they had to bond vocally and emotionally. The four girl bands and two boy bands embraced the challenge!

Later on, Gary, Kelly and Tulisa arrived to see how the newly formed groups were getting on. Everyone was hoping that the next day would bring great things.

61 STILL STANDING

BOOTCAMP BUZZ

John Wilding reached the Judges' Houses in 2010 but didn't get through to the Live Shows.

BOOTCAMP
DAY FOUR

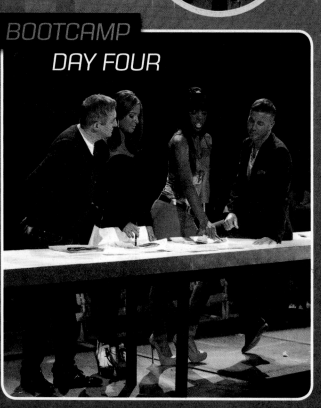

The final performance day had arrived! Today the contestants had to impress not only the four Judges, but also a live audience of thousands. Outside Wembley Arena, eager fans were queuing up in the rain, waiting for a chance to see the Judges and guess who would be the winner of *The X Factor 2011*.

The contestants were given a list of thirty songs. Their final challenge was to choose one song and make it their own. They were encouraged to give an individual performance, and could choose whether to sing without music or be accompanied by a piano, a guitar or a backing track.

SHEILA O'SULLIVAN

"One of the toughest weeks of my life."

Sheila gave an understated performance that matched her song choice well.

INTRODUCTION   JUDGES / PRESENTER PROFILES   RELEASING YOUR X FACTOR   THE NEXT STEPS   AUDITIONS

JOHN ADAMS

"Hopefully it'll be a polished performance."

John's version of 'Nobody Knows' showed his individual style, but would he be versatile enough for the show?

Meanwhile, Wembley Arena was filling up! A big blue **X** filled the screen at the back of the stage, and a gleaming black grand piano was wheeled into position. A family group took up a whole row, each wearing a 'Luke Lucas Fan Club' T-shirt. Another supporter was holding up a 'Misha Bryan' banner. Everyone knew that this was the make-or-break moment for the contestants.

Then the big **X** turned red, and the Judges walked out in a blaze of lights and music. The final challenge of Bootcamp was about to begin!

BOOTCAMP CHALLENGE 2
SONG LIST

'ANGEL' by Sarah McLachlan
'BEGGIN'' by Madcon
'BETTER' by Tom Baxter
'CANNONBALL' by Damien Rice
'CRY ME OUT' by Pixie Lott
'DYNAMITE' by Taio Cruz
'EVERYBODY HURTS' by R.E.M.
'FEELING GOOD' by Muse / Various
'GRENADE' by Bruno Mars
'I DON'T WANT TO MISS A THING' by Aerosmith
'IRIS' by The Goo Goo Dolls
'ONE' by U2
'KISS FROM A ROSE' by Seal
'MEET ME HALFWAY' by The Black Eyed Peas
'NEED YOU NOW' by Lady Antebellum
'NOBODY KNOWS' by Pink
'ROLLING IN THE DEEP' by Adele
'RULE THE WORLD' by Take That
'SKINNY LOVE' by Birdy
'SURVIVOR' by Destiny's Child
'SWEET CHILD O' MINE' by The Trees / Guns and Roses
'THE EDGE OF GLORY' by Lady Gaga
'THE FIRST CUT IS THE DEEPEST' by Sheryl Crow / Various
'TRUE COLOURS' by Cyndi Lauper / Eva Cassidy
'UNFAITHFUL' by Rihanna
'WHEN I GROW UP' by The Pussycat Dolls
'WHEN LOVE TAKES OVER' by David Guetta feat. Kelly Rowland
'WHEREVER YOU WILL GO' by The Calling
'YEAH 3X' by Chris Brown
'YOUR SONG' by Ellie Goulding / Elton John

CONTESTANTS' SONG CHOICES

AIESHA PEASE
UNFAITHFUL (Piano)

SARAH WATSON
CRY ME OUT/ROLLING IN THE DEEP (Guitar)

THE KEYS
ROLLING IN THE DEEP/DYNAMITE (Backing Track)

KIRSTY BANCROFT
KISS FROM A ROSE (Backing Track)

LASCEL WOOD
ANGEL (Piano)

CHRISSIE PITT
ONE (Backing Track)

JOHNNY ROBINSON
FEELING GOOD (Backing Track)

JOHN WILDING
WHEN LOVE TAKES OVER (Backing Track)

KENDRO
WHEN I GROW UP (Backing Track)

CRAIG COLTON
CANNONBALL (Guitar)

SAMANTHA BROOKES
GRENADE (Backing Track)

NATASHA ZIMBARO
UNFAITHFUL (Backing Track)

FRANCIS CARDOSA
SURVIVOR (Guitar)

MICHELLE BARRETT
ONE (Guitar)

4 REAL
YEAH 3X (Piano)

JADE RICHARDS
NOBODY KNOWS (Piano)

SIAN PHILLIPS
FEELING GOOD (Piano)

SCOTT FLANNERY
ONE (Guitar)

ESKIMO SMILE
WHEREVER YOU WILL GO (Guitar)

SOPHIE BOND
EVERYBODY HURTS (Backing Track)

FRANKIE COCOZZA
IRIS (Guitar)

NICOLE SIMPSON
NOBODY KNOWS (Piano)

TERRY WINSTANLEY
ONE (Guitar)

NIALL SEXTON
NOBODY KNOWS (Piano)

2 SHOES
BEGGIN' (Backing Track)

MELANIE MCCABE
FEELING GOOD (Piano)

JOSEPH GILLIGAN
I Don't Want to Miss a Thing (Piano)

GOLDIE CHEUNG
FEELING GOOD (Piano)

CAROLYNNE POOLE
EVERYBODY HURTS (Guitar)

JONJO KERR
IRIS (Guitar)

V-BOX
RULE THE WORLD (Piano)

AMELIA LILY
NOBODY KNOWS (Backing Track)

MISHA BRYAN
SURVIVOR (Piano)

JOE COX
IRIS (Piano)

BROOKLYN
KISS FROM A ROSE (Piano)

SHELIA O'SULLIVAN
ANGEL (Piano)

MARCUS COLLINS
KISS FROM A ROSE (Piano)

BASIL SIMON
BETTER (Backing Track)

GEMMA MCDOWALL
EDGE OF GLORY (Piano)

LEMUEL KNIGHTS
WHEN LOVE TAKES OVER (Guitar)

KITTY BRUCKNELL
FEELING GOOD (Backing Track)

CHELSEA REDFERN
TRUE COLOURS (Piano)

ESTRELLA
FEELING GOOD (Piano)

DAVID WILDER
EDGE OF GLORY (Guitar)

LUKE LUCAS
YEAH 3X (Backing Track)

CHELSEA SIANGA
FEELING GOOD (Backing Track)

VIBA
GRENADE (Piano)

NATHALIE MAKOMA
AEROSMITH (Guitar)

LOVETTES
WHEN LOVE TAKES OVER (Piano)

CANDICE BARON
FEELING GOOD (Backing Track)

MAX VICKERS
BEGGIN' (Guitar)

SOPHIE HABIBIS
SKINNY LOVE (Piano)

JOHN ADAMS
NOBODY KNOWS (Backing Track)

RHYTHMIX
YEAH 3X (Guitar)

CELESTE WAITE
BEGGIN' (Guitar)

JAMES MICHAEL
FIRST CUT IS THE DEEPEST (Guitar)

ORION
YEAH 3X (Backing Track)

FAUX PAS
SURVIVOR (Guitar)

HOLLY REPTON
GRENADE (Piano)

MISFITS
TRUE COLOURS (Guitar)

GIRL V BOY
WHEN LOVE TAKES OVER (Backing Track)

BOOTCAMP
DAY FIVE

It was the day of reckoning, and the contestants returned to Wembley Arena to find out who had earned a place in the Judges' Houses stage. There were just eight places in each category, and many people would be going home disappointed.

Only seven groups were good enough to win a place. To make up the eighth group, the Judges called back Jade Thirwell, Leigh-Anne Pinnock, Perrie Edwards and Jessy Nelson.

They were formed into a new band, and they chose the name Infinite Base for their Bootcamp performance, later changing it to Rhythmix.

As the final thirty-two acts celebrated, it was time for the Judges to find out which categories they would be mentoring!

GARY
BOYS

KELLY
GIRLS

TULISA
GROUPS

LOUIS
OVER 25s

JUDGES' HOUSES

GARY

The boys in Gary's category jetted off to LA for a taste of the high life!

The eight guys were overjoyed to discover that Gary was their mentor, and they were eager to prove themselves to him. Each contestant would sing two songs, and then Gary would have the difficult job of deciding their fate.

Between the rehearsals and the performances there was time for a bit of fun. The eight contestants strolled around LA, did the Walk of Fame and shared rooftop drinks with Gary like true superstars. They even found time for some ball games on the beach! But soon enough it was time to perform for Gary and Guest Mentor Robbie Williams, and the nerves started to kick in.

The boys poured their passions and hopes into their performances, and it wasn't easy for Gary to choose which acts he would be taking with him to the Live Shows. However, at last the moment arrived, and Gary took his place beside the pool in the sunshine to deliver the news . . .

Luke Lucas
Age: 16
Home town: Kent
Job: Student

"I did not expect anything like that."

JUDGES' HOUSES FAST FACTS

LOCATION: Los Angeles

CATEGORY: Boys

GUEST MENTOR:
Robbie Williams

CONTESTANTS:

Frankie Cocozza

Luke Lucas

Joe Cox

Craig Colton

Max Vickers

Marcus Collins

James Michael

John Wilding

"Will people vote for him?"

Joe Cox
Age: 17
Home town: Upminster, Essex
Job: Student

JUDGES' HOUSES
GARY

Max Vickers
Age: 19
Home town: Stockton-on-Tees
Job: Student / Children's Entertainer

"You need to work on stage presence."

"You have a beautiful gift."

John Wilding
Age: 18
Home town: Epping, Essex
Job: Student

BOYS SONG LIST

FRANKIE COCOZZA
'What's My Name'
'The A Team'

LUKE LUCAS
'Impossible'
'Billionaire'

JOE COX
'Knockin' on Heaven's Door'
'Jar of Hearts'

CRAIG COLTON
'Halo'
'Hold It Against Me'

MAX VICKERS
'The Only Exception'
'Issues'

MARCUS COLLINS
'One Big Family'
'Rolling in the Deep'

JAMES MICHAEL
'Perfect'
'Skinny Love'

JOHN WILDING
'Promise This'
'Edge of Glory'

LOS ANGELES LOWDOWN

Home to Hollywood and a host of stars, LA was the perfect venue for Gary's stars-in-the-making. It is known as the entertainment capital of the world, and tourists flock here to soak up the star-studded atmosphere. It also hosts the Academy Awards every year . . . time to roll out the red carpet, guys!

THROUGH TO THE LIVE SHOWS...

Frankie Cocozza

Craig Colton

James Michael

Marcus Collins

JUDGES' HOUSES

KELLY

Kelly took the girls to Miami to soak up some sunshine as they faced their final challenge.

The girls had come a long way since their first Auditions, but now their job was about to get even tougher. As one of the most successful singers in the world, Kelly knew exactly what she was looking for.

Kelly and her Guest Mentor Jennifer Hudson had to choose the four contestants who would have the best chance of making it to the Final. They were looking for versatility, personality and, above all, talent.

The contestants took some time out for drinks with Kelly at a beach bar. They even went down Ocean Drive in a Cadillac, which made them feel like superstars! But although they had fun, this wasn't a holiday. Soon they would be facing Kelly to find out if they had done enough to stay in the competition.

Kelly thought long and hard about who she would take to the Live Shows, and at last she was ready to reveal her decision. Which of the girls had proved they were worthy of this incredible opportunity?

INTRODUCTION   JUDGES / PRESENTER PROFILES   RELEASING YOUR X FACTOR   THE NEXT STEPS   AUDITIONS

Jade Richards
Age: 20
Home town: Fife, Scotland
Job: Photographic Student

"We have such high hopes for her."

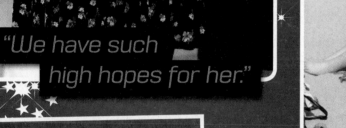

JUDGES' HOUSES
FAST FACTS

LOCATION: **Miami**

CATEGORY: **Girls**

GUEST MENTOR:
Jennifer Hudson

CONTESTANTS:
Jade Richards

Sophie Habibis

Misha Bryan

Melanie McCabe

Holly Repton

Amelia Lily

Sarah Watson

Janet Devlin

"I think she is phenomenal."

Melanie McCabe
Age: 18
Home town: Dublin
Job: Student

JUDGES' HOUSES
KELLY

Holly Repton
Age: 16
Home town: Oldham, Lancs
Job: Student

"You have a twang in there that is funky."

Sarah Watson
Age: 16
Home town: Wakefield
Job: Student

"She has a really pretty voice... she is exciting to listen to"

GIRLS SONG LIST

JADE RICHARDS
'You Don't Know Me'
'I Can't Make You Love Me'

SOPHIE HABIBIS
'He Won't Go'
'Come Away with Me'

MISHA BRYAN
'No More Drama'
'Crazy'

MELANIE MCCABE
'Grenade'
'I'll Be There'

HOLLY REPTON
'Just Can't Get Enough'
'For the First Time'

AMELIA LILY
'Fix You'
'E.T.'

SARAH WATSON
'Knock You Down'
'Sunday Morning'

JANET DEVLIN
'Cosmic Love'
'Beautiful'

MIAMI LOWDOWN

Miami sits on the Atlantic coast in Florida. Its beaches, festivals and events bring millions of visitors to the city every year, and it has been ranked as the richest city in America. It's a major TV production centre, and a dream setting for superstars!

THROUGH TO THE LIVE SHOWS...

Janet Devlin

Sophie Habibis

Amelia Lily

Misha Bryan

JUDGES' HOUSES
TULISA

Tulisa whisked the Groups away to the Greek island of Mykonos to soak up the sun while they worked.

The Groups were thrilled to have been chosen for Judges' Houses, and they knew that everything depended on how well they performed during their stay. Each group was desperate to reach the Live Shows, but only four of them would see their dreams come true.

The contestants took some time out to have lunch with Tulisa's grandmother. They walked beside the marina and visited the beach. However, they knew that Tulisa would only choose the most dedicated and determined acts for the Live Shows. They all had a lot to prove, so most of their time was spent rehearsing and developing their vocals.

With the help of Guest Mentor Jessie J, Tulisa listened carefully to each performance. They thought hard about which acts had shown the most talent, focus and potential. At last Tulisa reached her decision, and prepared to deliver the news to the eight groups.

INTRODUCTION — JUDGES / PRESENTER PROFILES — RELEASING YOUR X FACTOR — THE NEXT STEPS — AUDITIONS

The Lovettes

Age: 20 to 22

**Home town:
Manchester / Birmingham**

**Job: Single Mum / Shop
Assistant / Student**

"They look good."

JUDGES' HOUSES
FAST FACTS

LOCATION: **Mykonos**

CATEGORY: **Groups**

GUEST MENTOR:
Jessie J

CONTESTANTS:

Estrella

Boy V Girl

2 Shoes

The Keys

Nu Vibe

The Risk

The Lovettes

Rhythmix

"Vocally you
are great."

Boy V Girl

Age: 21 & 20

Home town: Manchester

Job: Beautician / Barber

JUDGES' HOUSES

TULISA

The Keys

Age: 24 to 26

Home town: Liverpool

Job: Unemployed / Marketing Manager / Model / Business Analyst

"You look like a band and sing like a band."

Estrella

Age: 21–26

Home town: Liverpool

Job: Beautician / Dental Nurse / Teaching Assistant / Fraud Officer

GROUPS SONG LIST

ESTRELLA
'Super Bass'
'Love The Way You Lie Part 2'

BOY V GIRL
'For The First Time'
'Use Somebody'

2 SHOES
'I Wanna Dance With Somebody'
'Tick Tock'

THE KEYS
'Best Thing I Never Had'
'Red'

NU VIBE
'Promise This'
'Written In The Stars'

THE RISK
'No Air'
'Man in The Mirror'

THE LOVETTES
'Forever Is Over'
'Who's that Chick'

RHYTHMIX
'Big Girls Don't Cry'
'Dynamite'

"Your vocals are all strong."

MYKONOS LOWDOWN

The island has become a magnet for celebrities and is a real party island. It is famous for its windmills and beautiful beaches. Tulisa's grandmother has a villa on the island and it's the perfect location for Tulisa to get to know the Groups.

THROUGH TO THE LIVE SHOWS...

Rhythmix

The Risk

2 Shoes

Nu Vibe

JUDGES' HOUSES
LOUIS

Louis took the Overs to beautiful Barcelona and treated them to a few days in the Spanish sun.

Having sailed through the Auditions and survived Bootcamp, Louis' eight contestants jetted off to Barcelona for their final challenge. While they were staying in the stunning hotel, they had to perform two songs and prove to Louis that they deserved a place in the Live Shows.

Louis and his Guest Mentor Sinitta listened as the contestants sang their hearts out. It was up to them to choose the four singers who would be most likely to take Louis all the way to the Final. This is always a difficult time for the Judges, but it's a decision that has to be made.

Of course, alongside the hard work Louis made sure that the contestants had some fun too. They tried out horse riding, walked down vibrant Las Ramblas and visited the famous cathedral. But their destiny was in Louis' hands, and they were longing to find out who would be given the chance to make their dreams come true.

Four of the contestants would be flying home to prepare for a life-changing experience – a place on the Live Shows of *The X Factor*. The other four contestants would be disappointed. The pressure was on, but who would rise to the challenge?

INTRODUCTION | JUDGES / PRESENTER PROFILES | RELEASING YOUR X FACTOR | THE NEXT STEPS | AUDITIONS

Terry Winstanley
Age: 51
Home town: Worthing, Sussex
Job: Scaffolder

"That blew me out the water."

JUDGES' HOUSES FAST FACTS

LOCATION: **Barcelona**

CATEGORY: **Over 25s**

GUEST MENTOR: **Sinitta**

CONTESTANTS:

Johnny Robinson

Kitty Brucknell

Carolynne Poole

Jonjo Kerr

Samantha Brookes

Terry Winstanley

Goldie Cheung

Joe Gilligan

"There is a great market for you."

Carolynne Poole
Age: 31
Home town: Huddersfield, Yorks
Job: Furniture Restorer

JUDGES'
HOUSES
LOUIS

Goldie Cheung
Age: 47
Home town: Lathom, Lancs
Job: Tai Chi Instructor

"You have great energy"

OVER 25s SONG LIST

JOHNNY ROBINSON
'Hot N Cold'
'Love Is a Losing Game'

KITTY BRUCKNELL
'Beautiful Disaster'
'Teenage Dream'

CAROLYNNE POOLE
'Need You Now'
'California King bed'

JONJO KERR
'One Day Like This'
'Don't You Remember'

SAMANTHA BROOKES
'Impossible'
'New York'

TERRY WINSTANLEY
'All by Myself'
'Handbags and Gladrags'

GOLDIE CHEUNG
'Addicted to Love'
'On the Floor'

JOE GILLIGAN
'Just the Way You Are'
'Beautiful'

"You have
a real talent."

Joe Gilligan
Age: 26
Home town: Withington
Job: Security Guard

BARCELONA LOWDOWN

Barcelona is one of the greatest cities in the world, with a fantastic cultural reputation and many beautiful sights. It is famous for the architectural work of Antoni Gaudí, and his unfinished church is a masterpiece. In addition, the city contains seven beaches and the central Las Ramblas Boulevard, which is always sparkling with life.

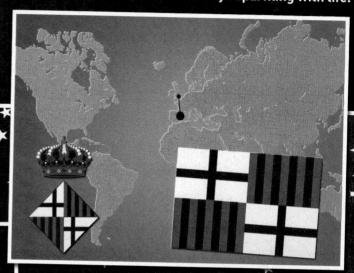

THROUGH TO THE LIVE SHOWS...

Jonjo Kerr

Kitty Brucknell

Samantha Brookes

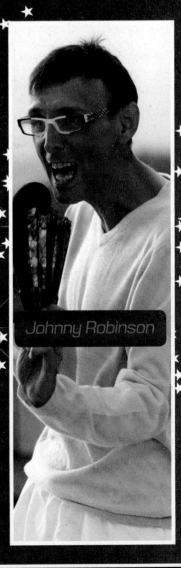

Johnny Robinson

THE X FACTOR

LIVE SHOW SCRAPBOOK

The next few pages give you the chance to keep your own personal record of your fave show. It's up to you how you use it . . .

Follow the shows live and fill in the pages as you watch, or use the scrapbook pages to record your memories of the highs and lows of each week in series eight. Check out *The X Factor* website for images, news and gossip. There's also space for you to stick in newspaper clippings about the Finalists.

As the acts are voted out week by week, you can keep your scrapbook up to date by using the red x stickers and placing them over those acts who have left the competition!

OUT

If you're feeling creative you could even rewrite history and plan an alternative version of the series. Make up what the Judges said and decide for yourself who stayed and who was eliminated!

However you use these pages, you will be able to keep them as a memento of the best series yet – the series where you became the fifth Judge!

CRAIG COLTON   FRANKIE COCOZZA   MARCUS COLLINS   JAMES MICHAEL   SOPHIE HABIBIS   MISHA BRYAN   AMELIA LILY   JANET DEVLIN

LIVE SHOWS

week 1

Theme:

Song choices

Craig Colton:

Frankie Cocozza:

Marcus Collins:

James Michael:

Sophie Habibis:

Misha Bryan:

Amelia Lily:

Janet Devlin:

2 Shoes:

Nu Vibe:

Rhythmix:

The Risk:

Johnny Robinson:

Kitty Brucknell:

Jonjo Kerr:

Samantha Brookes:

Score out of 10

What would you have worn?

What would you have sung?

who was your favourite?

WHO'S SINGING FOR SURVIVAL?

Acts:

Song Choice:

Who did the Judges vote to stay?

Gary:

Louis:

Kelly:

Tulisa:

If the vote went to DEADLOCK, place the sticker here!

who left the show?

THIS WEEK'S GUEST ACT

Use this space to stick in your favourite X Factor pictures of the week.

There are lots of images of all the contestants and Judges at www.itv.com/xfactor

You'll also find lots of pictures in newspapers and magazines.

09847007348   POLAROID©92

Did you agree?

2 SHOES   NU VIBE   RHYTHMIX   THE RISK   JOHNNY ROBINSON   KITTY BRUCKNELL   JONJO KERR   SAMANTHA BROOKES

LIVE SHOWS

week 2

Theme:

Use this space to stick in your favourite X Factor pictures of the week.

There are lots of images of all the contestants and Judges at

www.itv.com/xfactor

You'll also find lots of pictures in newspapers and magazines.

Who improved most since week 1?

THE X FACTOR

Which Judge has the best category?

Who had the best songs?

Song choices

Score out of 10

Craig Colton:

Frankie Cocozza:

Marcus Collins:

James Michael:

Sophie Habibis:

Misha Bryan:

Amelia Lily:

Janet Devlin:

2 Shoes:

Nu Vibe:

Rhythmix:

The Risk:

Johnny Robinson:

Kitty Brucknell:

Jonjo Kerr:

Samantha Brookes:

WHO'S SINGING FOR SURVIVAL?

Acts: Song Choice:

Who did the Judges vote to stay?

Gary: Louis:

Kelly: Tulisa:

If the vote went to DEADLOCK, place the sticker here!

who left the show?

Did you agree?

THIS WEEK'S GUEST ACT

CRAIG COLTON   FRANKIE COCOZZA   MARCUS COLLINS   JAMES MICHAEL   SOPHIE HABIBIS   MISHA BRYAN   AMELIA LILY   JANET DEVLIN

LIVE SHOWS

week 3

Theme: _____

Which Judge do you most respect?

Which Finalist would you be friends with?

Who has the most natural talent?

Song choices

Craig Colton: _____

Frankie Cocozza: _____

Marcus Collins: _____

James Michael: _____

Sophie Habibis: _____

Misha Bryan: _____

Amelia Lily: _____

Janet Devlin: _____

2 Shoes: _____

Nu Vibe: _____

Rhythmix: _____

The Risk: _____

Johnny Robinson: _____

Kitty Brucknell: _____

Jonjo Kerr: _____

Samantha Brookes: _____

Score out of 10

WHO'S SINGING FOR SURVIVAL?

Acts:

Song Choice:

Who did the Judges vote to stay?

Gary: _____

Louis: _____

Kelly: _____

Tulisa: _____

If the vote went to DEADLOCK, place the sticker here!

who left the show?

THIS WEEK'S GUEST ACT

Use this space to stick in your favourite X Factor pictures of the week.

There are lots of images of all the contestants and Judges at

www.itv.com/xfactor

You'll also find lots of pictures in newspapers and magazines.

Did you agree?

2 SHOES

NU VIBE

RHYTHMIX

THE RISK

JOHNNY ROBINSON

KITTY BRUCKNELL

JONJO KERR

SAMANTHA BROOKES

LIVE SHOWS

week 4

Use this space to stick in your favourite X Factor pictures of the week.

There are lots of images of all the contestants and Judges at www.itv.com/xfactor

You'll also find lots of pictures in newspapers and magazines.

POLAROID032

THE X FACTOR

Who surprised you?

Who disappointed you?

Who had the best hairstyle?

Theme:

Song choices

Score out of 10

Craig Colton:

Frankie Cocozza:

Marcus Collins:

James Michael:

Sophie Habibis:

Misha Bryan:

Amelia Lily:

Janet Devlin:

2 Shoes:

Nu Vibe:

Rhythmix:

The Risk:

Johnny Robinson:

Kitty Brucknell:

Jonjo Kerr:

Samantha Brookes:

WHO'S SINGING FOR SURVIVAL?

Acts:

Song Choice:

Who did the Judges vote to stay?

Gary:

Louis:

Kelly:

Tulisa:

If the vote went to DEADLOCK, place the sticker here!

who left the show?

Did you agree?

THIS WEEK'S GUEST ACT

CRAIG COLTON · FRANKIE COCOZZA · MARCUS COLLINS · JAMES MICHAEL · SOPHIE HABIBIS · MISHA BRYAN · AMELIA LILY · JANET DEVLIN

LIVE SHOWS

week 5

Theme:

What's your dream theme?

Who's had the toughest week?

Who has shown the most improvement?

Song choices

Craig Colton:

Frankie Cocozza:

Marcus Collins:

James Michael:

Sophie Habibis:

Misha Bryan:

Amelia Lily:

Janet Devlin:

2 Shoes:

Nu Vibe:

Rhythmix:

The Risk:

Johnny Robinson:

Kitty Brucknell:

Jonjo Kerr:

Samantha Brookes:

Score out of 10

WHO'S SINGING FOR SURVIVAL?

Acts: Song Choice:

Who did the Judges vote to stay?

Gary: Louis:

Kelly: Tulisa:

who left the show?

If the vote went to DEADLOCK, place the sticker here!

THIS WEEK'S GUEST ACT

Use this space to stick in your favourite X Factor pictures of the week.

There are lots of images of all the contestants and Judges at

www.itv.com/xfactor

You'll also find lots of pictures in newspapers and magazines.

Did you agree?

2 SHOES

NU VIBE

RHYTHMIX

THE RISK

JOHNNY ROBINSON

KITTY BRUCKNELL

JONJO KERR

SAMANTHA BROOKES

95

LIVE SHOWS

week 6

Use this space to stick in your favourite X Factor pictures of the week.

There are lots of images of all the contestants and Judges at www.itv.com/xfactor

You'll also find lots of pictures in newspapers and magazines.

Who do you think should have left?

THE X FACTOR

Theme:

Song choices

Song choices	Score out of 10
Craig Colton:	
Frankie Cocozza:	
Marcus Collins:	
James Michael:	
Sophie Habibis:	
Misha Bryan:	
Amelia Lily:	
Janet Devlin:	
2 Shoes:	
Nu Vibe:	
Rhythmix:	
The Risk:	
Johnny Robinson:	
Kitty Brucknell:	
Jonjo Kerr:	
Samantha Brookes:	

Who deserved a second chance?

Which Finalist put on the best show?

WHO'S SINGING FOR SURVIVAL?

Acts: Song Choice:

Who did the Judges vote to stay?

Gary: _____   Louis: _____

Kelly: _____   Tulisa: _____

If the vote went to DEADLOCK, place the sticker here!

who left the show?

Did you agree?

THIS WEEK'S GUEST ACT

CRAIG COLTON · FRANKIE COCOZZA · MARCUS COLLINS · JAMES MICHAEL · SOPHIE HABIBIS · MISHA BRYAN · AMELIA LILY · JANET DEVLIN

LIVE SHOWS

week 7

How would you sum up week 7?

Who would you like to see as a Guest Mentor?

Which Judge did you agree with?

Theme:

Song choices

	Score out of 10
Craig Colton:	○
Frankie Cocozza:	○
Marcus Collins:	○
James Michael:	○
Sophie Habibis:	○
Misha Bryan:	○
Amelia Lily:	○
Janet Devlin:	○
2 Shoes:	○
Nu Vibe:	○
Rhythmix:	○
The Risk:	○
Johnny Robinson:	○
Kitty Brucknell:	○
Jonjo Kerr:	○
Samantha Brookes:	○

WHO'S SINGING FOR SURVIVAL?

Acts: _____   Song Choice: _____

Who did the Judges vote to stay?

Gary: _____   Louis: _____

Kelly: _____   Tulisa: _____

who left the show?

If the vote went to DEADLOCK, place the sticker here!

THIS WEEK'S GUEST ACT

Use this space to stick in your favourite X Factor pictures of the week.

There are lots of images of all the contestants and Judges at

www.itv.com/xfactor

You'll also find lots of pictures in newspapers and magazines.

09847007348   POLAROID

Did you agree?

2 SHOES

NU VIBE

RHYTHMIX

THE RISK

JOHNNY ROBINSON

KITTY BRUCKNELL

JONJO KERR

SAMANTHA BROOKES

LIVE SHOWS

week 8

Theme:

Use this space to stick in your favourite X Factor pictures of the week.

There are lots of images of all the contestants and Judges at www.itv.com/xfactor

You'll also find lots of pictures in newspapers and magazines.

POLAROID051

THE X FACTOR

Who is coping best with the pressure?

Who has the most star quality?

How would you stand out from the crowd?

Song choices

Score out of 10

Craig Colton:

Frankie Cocozza:

Marcus Collins:

James Michael:

Sophie Habibis:

Misha Bryan:

Amelia Lily:

Janet Devlin:

2 Shoes:

Nu Vibe:

Rhythmix:

The Risk:

Johnny Robinson:

Kitty Brucknell:

Jonjo Kerr:

Samantha Brookes:

WHO'S SINGING FOR SURVIVAL?

Acts: Song Choice:

Who did the Judges vote to stay?

Gary: _____   Louis: _____

Kelly: _____   Tulisa: _____

If the vote went to DEADLOCK, place the sticker here!

who left the show?

Did you agree?

THIS WEEK'S GUEST ACT

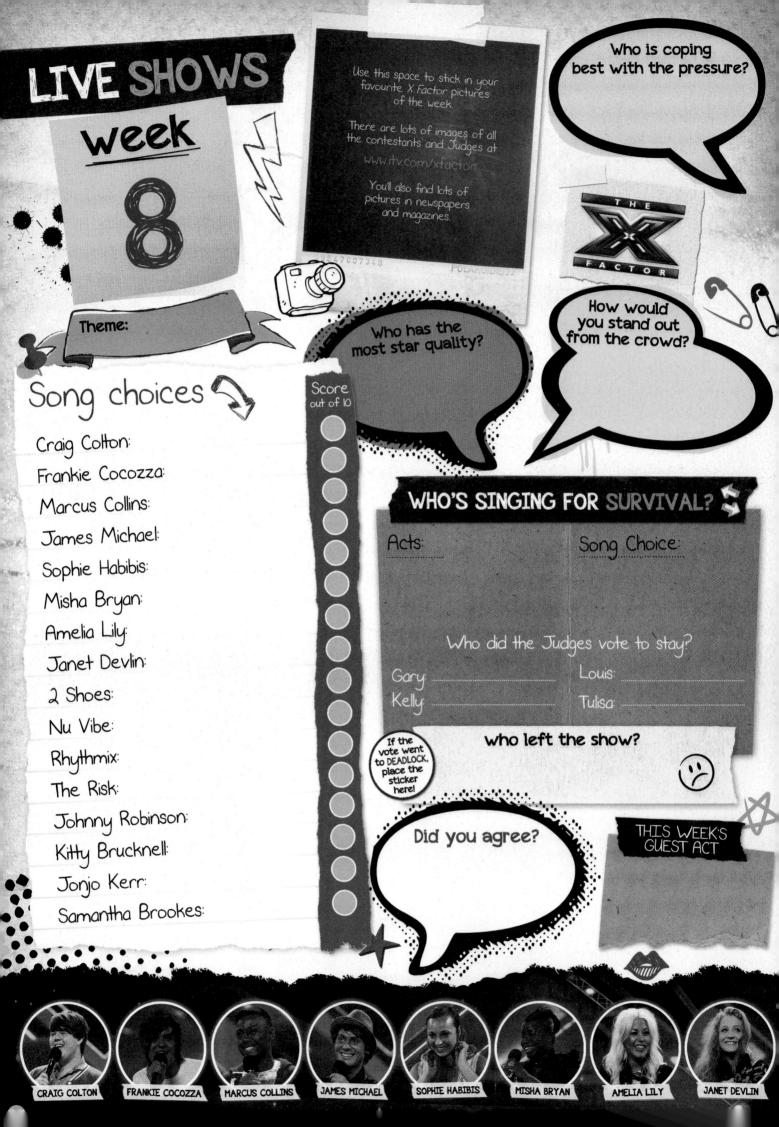

CRAIG COLTON   FRANKIE COCOZZA   MARCUS COLLINS   JAMES MICHAEL   SOPHIE HABIBIS   MISHA BRYAN   AMELIA LILY   JANET DEVLIN

LIVE SHOWS

week 9

What was your fave outift?

What was the best song choice?

Who was your winner?

Theme:

Song choices

Craig Colton:

Frankie Cocozza:

Marcus Collins:

James Michael:

Sophie Habibis:

Misha Bryan:

Amelia Lily:

Janet Devlin:

2 Shoes:

Nu Vibe:

Rhythmix:

The Risk:

Johnny Robinson:

Kitty Brucknell:

Jonjo Kerr:

Samantha Brookes:

Score out of 10

WHO'S SINGING FOR SURVIVAL?

Acts:

Song Choice:

Who did the Judges vote to stay?

Gary: _____ Louis: _____

Kelly: _____ Tulisa: _____

If the vote went to DEADLOCK, place the sticker here!

who left the show?

THIS WEEK'S GUEST ACT

Use this space to stick in your favourite X Factor pictures of the week.

There are lots of images of all the contestants and Judges at

www.itv.com/xfactor

You'll also find lots of pictures in newspapers and magazines.

09847007348   POLAROID

Did you agree?

2 SHOES   NU VIBE   RHYTHMIX   THE RISK   JOHNNY ROBINSON   KITTY BRUCKNELL   JONJO KERR   SAMANTHA BROOKES

LIVE SHOWS

week 10

Act	Song Choices	GIVE A SCORE FOR EACH SONG out of 10

Themes:

Guest act(s)

What was the highlight of the Final?

Who did the crowd like best?

Who did you vote for?

ENJOY THE FINAL!

CRAIG COLTON

FRANKIE COCOZZA

MARCUS COLLINS

JAMES MICHAEL

SOPHIE HABIBIS

MISHA BRYAN

AMELIA LILY

JANET DEVLIN

The X Factor star spotter

Use this space to stick in your favourite X Factor pictures of the week.

There are lots of images of all the contestants and Judges at

www.itv.com/xfactor

You'll also find lots of pictures in newspapers and magazines.

POLAROID@32
09847007348

★The★Winner★

09847007348
POLAROID@32

09847007348
POLAROID@32

Who were the runners up?

If the vote went to DEADLOCK, place the sticker here!

Which Judge had the winning act?

AND THE X FACTOR WINNER IS...

Memorable quote from a Judge...

Memorable quote from The X Factor Winner...

Do you agree with the final result?

2 SHOES

NU VIBE

RHYTHMIX

THE RISK

JOHNNY ROBINSON

KITTY BRUCKNELL

JONJO KERR

SAMANTHA BROOKES

LIVE SHOWS

Matt Cardle playing the guitar in the Final, who this year can play an instrument?

Matt Cardle being announced winner of 2010, who do you think will be crowned this year's winner of The X Factor

After thousands of Auditions, a gruelling Bootcamp and a nerve-wracking time at Judges' Houses, the sixteen Finalists of 2011 are ready to face the Live Shows.

They have already been on an incredible journey, and yet this is just the beginning. Ahead of them lie ten weeks of hard work, excitement, criticism and fame. All sixteen share a dream of being crowned winner, but only one act can emerge victorious.

The Judges are also at the beginning of a new adventure. For Gary, Kelly and Tulisa it is the first time that they have faced the high drama of the Live Shows. All four Judges are

Cher performing song in week 9, who do you think will be the best dancer this year?

Rebecca Ferguson singing in the Final, who do you think will make it to the Final Show?

hoping that someone from their own category will win the competition.

The Live Shows are great fun, but they are also incredibly demanding, and not everyone will be able to handle the pressure. Week after week, the numbers will dwindle and the challenges will become harder. Only one of the final sixteen acts has the talent, strength and determination to make it all the way to the top. Who will it be?

One Direction waiting for the Judges' comments the Final, which Judges' comments do you generally agree with most?

Matt Cardle singing in the Final, will this year's winner be from the Boys, Girls, Over 25s or the Groups?

Who do you think will win *The X Factor 2011*

Craig's put his day job on hold while he works hard to follow his dream.

Craig told his parents that he had got tickets for the show, but he had to work and couldn't go. So his mum and dad were sitting in the audience when he walked out on stage. They could hardly believe their eyes!

When Craig began to sing, the unusual tone of his voice wowed the audience. People rose to their feet, and as the final notes rang out he got a standing ovation.

After shining at Bootcamp and at the Judges' Houses stage, Craig was given the chance to fulfil his ambitions. Can he make it all the way to the Final?

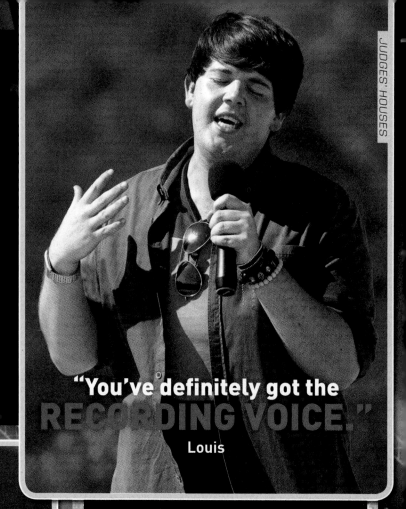

"You've definitely got the **RECORDING VOICE.**"

Louis

"It was **MESMORISING."**

Gary

Profile

Age:	22
Home Town:	Kirby, Wirrall
Job:	Student / Shop Assistant
Audition City:	Liverpool
Mentor:	Gary

Audition song:
'Hiding My Heart'

Bootcamp songs:
'Born This Way'
'Cannonball'

Judges' Houses songs:
'Halo'
'Hold It Against Me'

CRAIG COLTON

THE BOYS

At his Audition, Frankie swaggered onto the stage looking supremely confident. He waved at the audience and grinned at the Judges. When Louis asked why he was there, his reply was simple. "To get loads of girls!"

Dressed simply in a white t-shirt and jeans, Frankie charmed and entertained the crowd. Girls were on their feet and dancing along, and the Judges were smiling. He headed off to Bootcamp with four yesses, and now he has the chance to experience the life of a superstar!

"He's good but he KNOWS IT!"
Tulisa

"We've NEVER had anyone like him before."
Louis

Profile

Age:	18
Home Town:	Brighton
Job:	Unemployed
Audition City:	London
Mentor:	Gary

Audition song:
'Valerie'

Bootcamp songs:
'Breakeven'
'Iris'

Judges' Houses songs:
'What's My Name'
'The A Team'

"I want to be FAMOUS"

FRANKIE COCOZZA

THE BOYS

James looked nervous and uncertain when he first appeared on *The X Factor* stage. With one hand tucked in his pocket, he broke effortlessly into his song, keeping his eyes closed and focusing on the music.

Three of the Judges were impressed, but Kelly proved harder to convince. With a no from Kelly but a yes from all the other Judges, James made his way to Bootcamp. There he proved that he had what it takes to stay in the competition! James made it into Gary's category and now faces the ultimate challenge of the Live Shows.

"That's the kind of vocal that **SELLS ALBUMS.**"
Tulisa

"**GREAT voice.**"
Gary

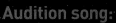

Profile

Age:	20
Home Town:	Widnes, Cheshire
Job:	Unemployed
Audition City:	Liverpool
Mentor:	Gary

Audition song:
'Make You Feel My Love'

Bootcamp songs:
'Breakeven'
'The First Cut Is The Deepest'

Judges' Houses songs:
'Perfect'
'Skinny Love'

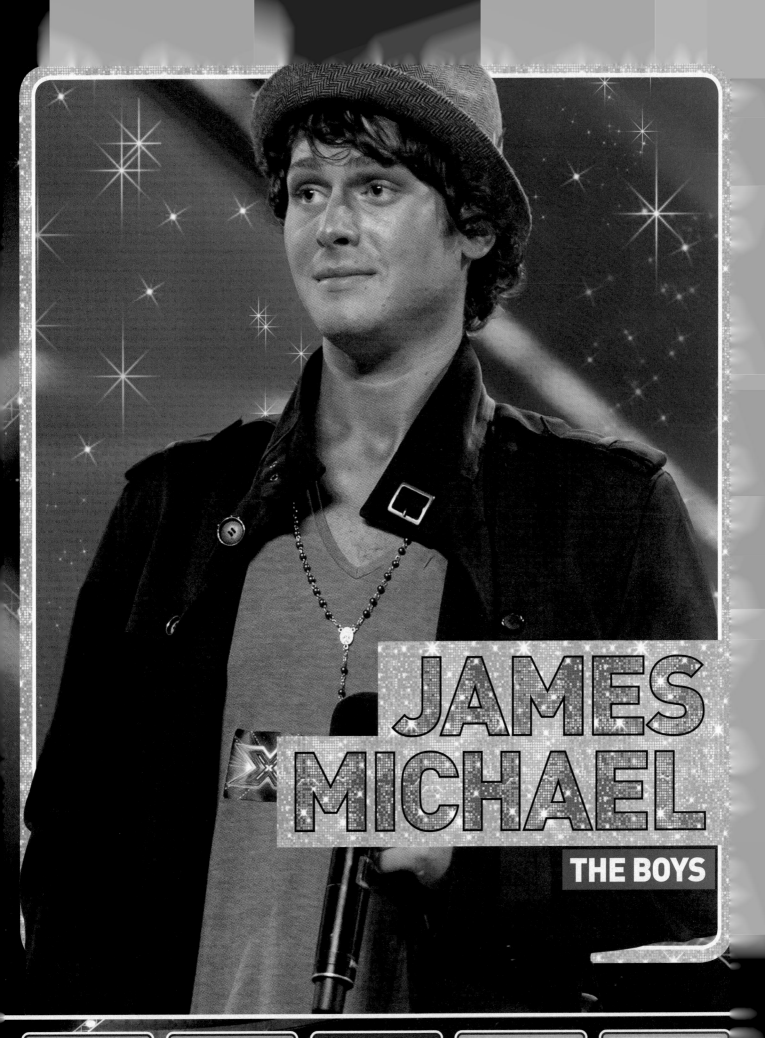

JAMES MICHAEL

THE BOYS

Marcus's clients call him the singing hairdresser, and he is pursuing his ambition to become a world-famous singer.

Dreaming of a better life for himself and his family, Marcus couldn't wait to start his Audition. As he stepped out in front of the excited Liverpool crowd, his eyes were sparkling with excitement. This was where he belonged!

Marcus's Audition had the Judges applauding, and the audience was even singing along. He headed for Bootcamp with four yesses.

Things didn't go quite as smoothly for him at Bootcamp, but Marcus made it to Judges' Houses. Now he has the chance to be in the Live Final!

"You were AMAZING TO WATCH."
Kelly

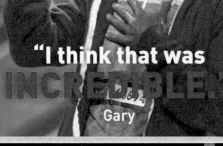

"I think that was INCREDIBLE."
Gary

Profile

Age:	23
Home Town:	Liverpool
Job:	Hairdresser
Audition City:	Liverpool
Mentor:	Gary

Audition song:
'Signed, Sealed, Delivered, I'm Yours'

Bootcamp songs:
'Born This Way'
'Kiss From A Rose'

Judges' Houses songs:
'One Big Family'
'Rolling in the Deep'

MARCUS COLLINS

THE BOYS

Sophie came to the Auditions wanting more from life than her job as a barmaid.

With four big yesses to boost her confidence, Sophie headed to Bootcamp. There her hard work paid off and she was taken forward to the Judges' Houses stage.

Kelly was impressed by Sophie's voice, and made her dreams come true by choosing her for the Live Shows. Now she has to prove to the nation that she deserves a place in the Final!

"WOW!"
Gary

"There is something about you that INTRIGUES me."
Tulisa

Profile

Age:	19
Home Town:	London
Job:	Barmaid
Audition City:	London
Mentor:	Kelly

Audition song:
'I Got Trouble' / 'Halo'

Bootcamp songs:
'You've Got The Love'
'Skinny Love'

Judges' Houses songs:
'He Won't Go'
'Come Away with Me'

SOPHIE HABIBIS

THE GIRLS

Misha has dreamed of being a professional singer since she was nine, and she thrived in the exciting atmosphere of the Auditions.

After her spectacular Audition, which included a rap that had everyone on their feet, Misha proved her star quality at Bootcamp. She was chosen to go through to the next stage, and she continued to shine at Kelly's house. Having been picked for the Live Shows, Misha can't wait for the next stage of the competition!

"You are going to GO FAR."
Louis

"She's a SURVIVOR, a FIGHTER."
Gary

Profile

Age:	19
Home Town:	Withington
Job:	Music Student
Audition City:	Manchester
Mentor:	Kelly

Audition song:
'Respect'

Bootcamp songs:
'Price Tag'
'Survivor'

Judges' Houses songs:
'No More Drama'
'Crazy'

MISHA BRYAN

THE GIRLS

Amelia turned up for her Audition supported by her family. She was thrilled at the thought of performing in front of thousands of people!

The Judges loved the energy and boldness of Amelia's Audition. The smiles on their faces told everyone that this girl was heading straight for Bootcamp.

With dreams of a future in the music industry, Amelia dazzled the Judges at Bootcamp and made it all the way through to the Live Shows. Everyone is excited to see how she will develop in the competition!

"You have a **BIG BEAUTIFUL VOICE.**"
Kelly

"I am **BLOWN AWAY.**"
Gary

Profile

Age:	16
Home Town:	Middlesbrough
Job:	Student
Audition City:	Liverpool
Mentor:	Kelly

Audition song:
'Piece of My Heart'

Bootcamp songs:
'You've Got The Love'
'Nobody Knows'

Judges' Houses songs:
'Fix You'
'E.T.'

AMELIA LILY

THE GIRLS

Janet spends a lot of time by herself, reading, writing and singing. She has been writing songs and poetry since she was seven-years-old, but the Audition was her first chance to see what an audience would think of her talent.

Shy and trembling, Janet stepped onto the Audition stage . . . and delivered a stunning performance! The purity and simplicity of her voice enchanted the audience and the Judges. A look of excitement and wonder passed over Gary's face as he listened.

After Janet received a standing ovation, her *X Factor* journey began. She was outstanding at Bootcamp and Judges' Houses, and now she faces the biggest challenge of all – the Live Shows. Will she develop the confidence she needs to be a worldwide recording artist?

"She's the
ONE TO BEAT."
Louis

Profile

Age:	16
Home Town:	Omagh, Co Tyrone
Job:	Student
Audition City:	Liverpool
Mentor:	Kelly

"Everything about her is so
BEAUTIFUL"
Gary

Audition song:
'Your Song'

Bootcamp songs:
'Breakeven'
'I Don't Want to Miss a Thing'

Judges' Houses songs:
'Cosmic Love'
'Beautiful'

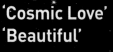

JANET DEVLIN

THE GIRLS

Lucy and Charley are massively excited to have the chance to be the first group to win *The X Factor*.

The girls are bubbly and full of fun, and the audience went wild for their first Audition.

They were well prepared and the Judges liked them. At Bootcamp they proved that they were prepared to work hard, and Tulisa was impressed by them in Greece.

"You have a
NICE BLEND."
Kelly

"I love the CHEMISTRY between the two of you."
Louis

Profile

Age:	21 & 23
Home Town:	London
Job:	Fragrance Shop Assistant / Telesales
Audition City:	London
Mentor:	Tulisa

Audition song:
'All My Life'

Bootcamp songs:
'Unfaithful'
'Beggin'

Judges' Houses songs:
'Dance With Somebody'
'Please Don't Leave Me'

222489

222488

2 SHOES

GROUPS

Ashford, Bradley, Stefan, Richard and Jordan Auditioned separately, and all made it through to Bootcamp. However, the Judges thought that they would do better in a group and chose to bring them together.

Nu Vibe impressed everyone with their determination and ability to blend with each other. At the Judges' Houses stage they worked hard to prove that they could succeed despite being such a new band.

FIRST AUDITION

FIRST AUDITION

Profile

Age:	16 - 19
Home Town:	Birmingham Liverpool London Manchester
Job:	Students
Audition City:	Birmingham Liverpool London Manchester
Mentor:	Tulisa

"The girls will LIKE YOU."
Tulisa

Audition song:
Group formed at Judges' Houses

Bootcamp songs:
Group formed at Judges' Houses

Judges' Houses songs:
'Promise This'
'Written In The Stars'

FIRST AUDITION

FIRST AUDITION

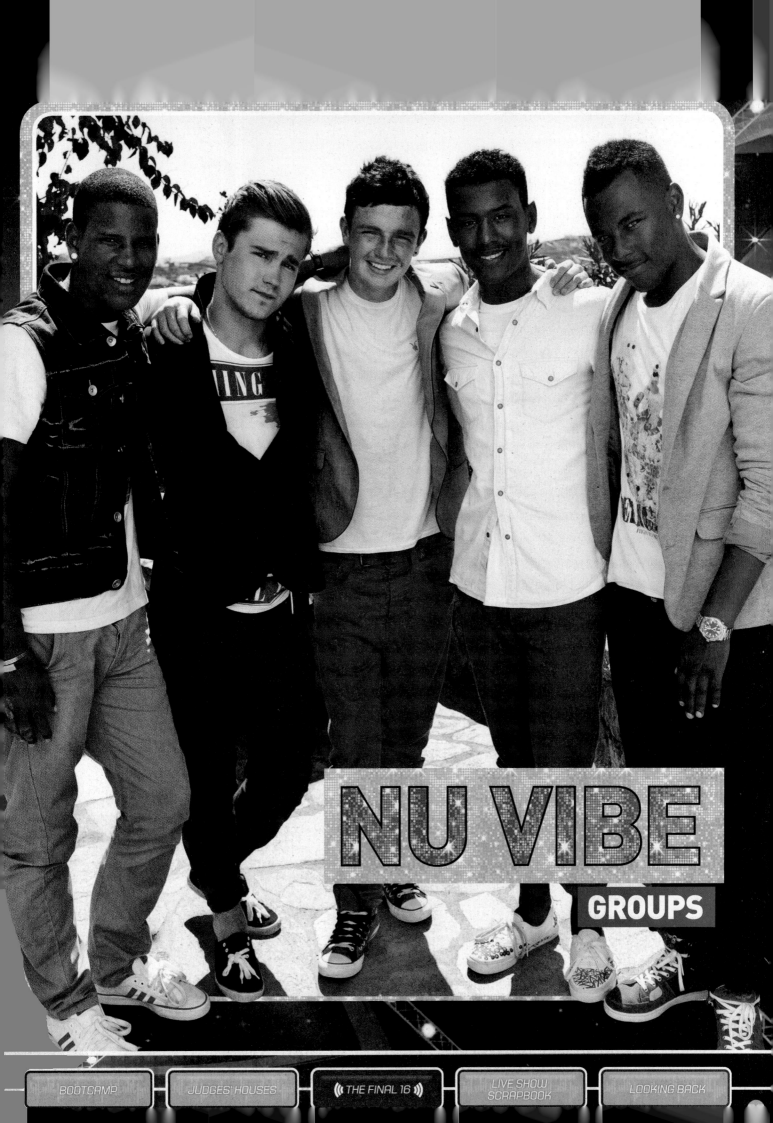

NU VIBE

GROUPS

The Rhythmix girls met each other at Bootcamp as solo artists. However, the Judges felt that each of them would work better in a group.

When Jesy, Perrie, Leigh-Anne and Jade began to sing together, the Judges agreed that something special had been created. They went through to Tulisa's house and she chose them for the Live Shows. Will they continue to prove that the new generation of Judges know how to put a band together?

Profile

Age:	**18 - 20**
Home Town:	**London** **Glasgow**
Job:	**Barmaid** **Waitress** **Student**
Audition City:	**London** **Glasgow**
Mentor:	**Tulisa**

"The group that didn't want to be a group were THE BEST."

Tulisa

Audition song:
Group formed at Judges' Houses

Bootcamp songs:
Group formed at Judges' Houses

Judges' Houses songs:
'Big Girls Don't Cry'
'Dynamite'

RHYTHMIX

GROUPS

The boys of The Risk Auditioned separately and were formed into a band by the Judges.

But further twists were coming for the lads! Marlon and Mitchell were taken out, and Charlie from The Keys joined the band. The Judges had a vision, and their faith was justified when Tulisa picked them for the Live Shows.

Profile

Age:	18 - 20
Home Town:	**London** **Manchester** **Liverpool**
Job:	**Car salesman** **Graduate** **Fast Food Worker** **Unemployed**
Audition City:	**London** **Manchester** **Liverpool**
Mentor:	**Tulisa**

"Were asking A LOT OF THEM."

Gary

Audition song:
Group formed at Judges' Houses

Bootcamp songs:
Group formed at Judges' Houses

Judges' Houses songs:
'No Air'
'Man In The Mirror'

THE RISK

GROUPS

Johnny has always dreamed of making an album and being a professional singer. Now those dreams have a chance of coming true as he takes his place as a Finalist on the glittering *X Factor* stage!

When Johnny told the Judges that he would like to be as big as Lady Gaga at his first Audition, there were a few raised eyebrows. But almost as soon as he started singing, people were jumping to their feet and cheering. The voice that came from his tiny frame blew them all away. Johnny was moved to tears – he could not have imagined a better reaction. Even the Judges were applauding!

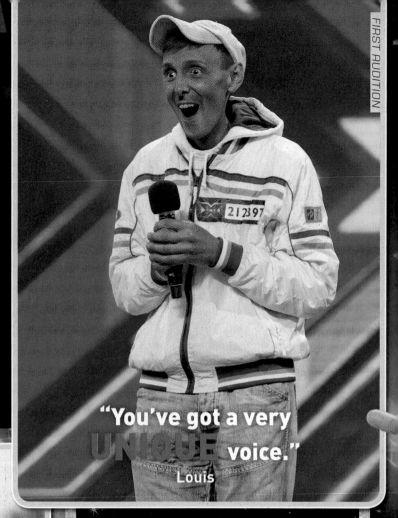

"You've got a very UNIQUE voice."
Louis

"I just thought that was an AMAZING Audition."
Gary

Profile

Age:	45
Home Town:	Harrow, London
Job:	Unemployed
Audition City:	London
Mentor:	Louis

Audition song:
'At Last'

Bootcamp songs:
'Firework'
'Feeling Good'

Judges' Houses songs:
'Hot N Cold'
'Love Is a Losing Game'

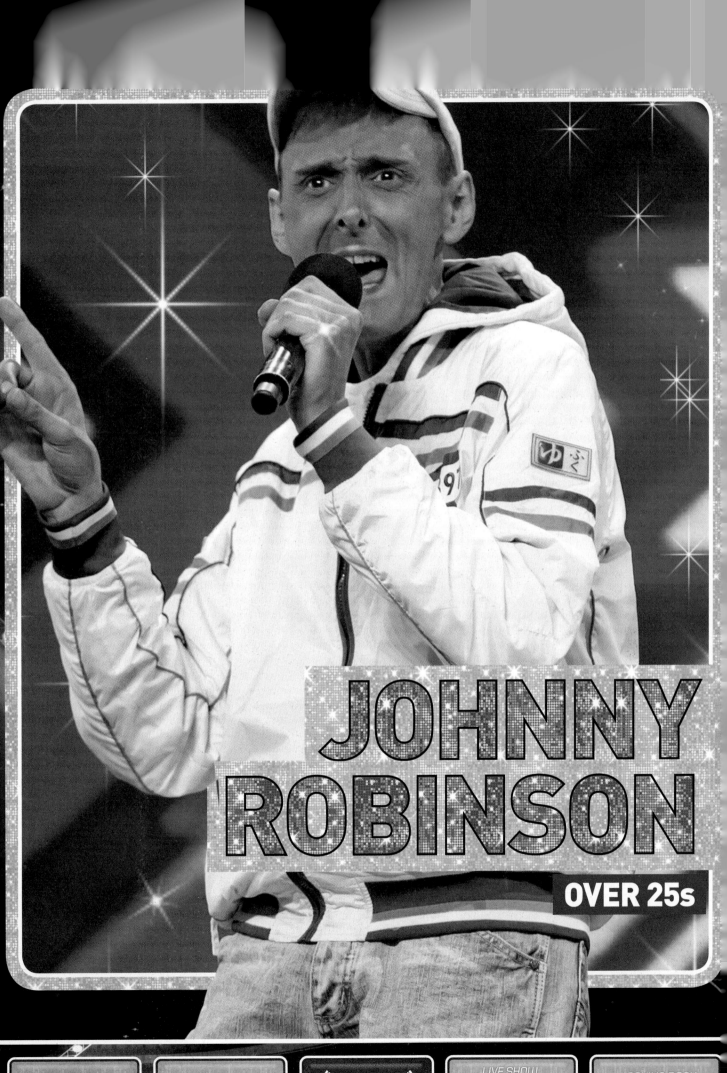

JOHNNY ROBINSON

OVER 25s

Kitty knows she can sing but wants people to like her as well.

From the moment she stepped on-stage, Kitty has worked hard to earn her place in the Live Shows. She has faced rejections and knock-backs, but after her Audition there was no doubt that she was full of potential. Her voice rang out over a hushed arena, and the audience gasped in amazement. Kitty's talent is obvious, but what will *The X Factor* make of her unique 'diva glam pop' style?

"WOW!"
Gary

Profile

Age:	26
Home Town:	Cheltenham, Glos.
Job:	Tribute Singer
Audition City:	London
Mentor:	Louis

"People will either **LOVE YOU** or **HATE YOU.**"
Tulisa

Audition song:
'**Edge of Glory**'

Bootcamp songs:
'**You've Got the Love**'
'**Feeling Good**'

Judges' Houses songs:
'**Beautiful Disaster**'
'**Teenage Dream**'

FIRST AUDITION

BOOTCAMP

KITTY BRUCKNELL

OVER 25s

Jonjo has always been a music fan, but it was his army colleagues who suggested that he should enter *The X Factor*. Three of them came along to support him, together with his wife and his son.

After a nervous start, Jonjo gave a good performance at his Audition. However, the Judges told him that he needed to work hard and start believing in himself. Jonjo took their words to heart and pushed himself at Bootcamp and at Louis' House. His hard work paid off, and he can't wait to perform in front of a national audience!

"You made us all EMOTIONAL."
Kelly

"A STAR has just been born."
Gary

Profile

Age:	27
Home Town:	Warminster, Wilts.
Job:	Soldier
Audition City:	Birmingham
Mentor:	Louis

Audition song:
'Handbags and Gladrags'

Bootcamp songs:
'Breakeven'
'Iris'

Judges' Houses songs:
'One Day Like This'
'Don't You Remember'

JONJO KERR

OVER 25s

Chatty Samantha gave a fantastic Audition – as soon as the Judges could get her to stop talking!

Samantha was shaking with nerves when she stepped onto the stage, but as soon as she started to sing she found her confidence. When the song finished, the Judges and the audience gave her a standing ovation.

The Judges raved about her personality and her voice, and Samantha could hardly believe it.

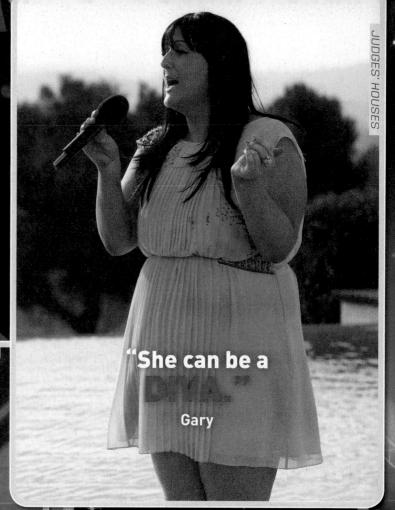

"She can be a DIVA."
Gary

"GREAT PERSONALITY and a GREAT VOICE"
Kelly

FIRST AUDITION

Profile

Age:	31
Home Town:	Rhyl, North Wales
Job:	Barmaid
Audition City:	Manchester
Mentor:	Louis

Audition song:
'One Moment In Time'

Bootcamp songs:
'Firework'
'Grenade'

Judges' Houses songs:
'Impossible'
'New York'

JUDGES' HOUSES

JUDGES' HOUSES

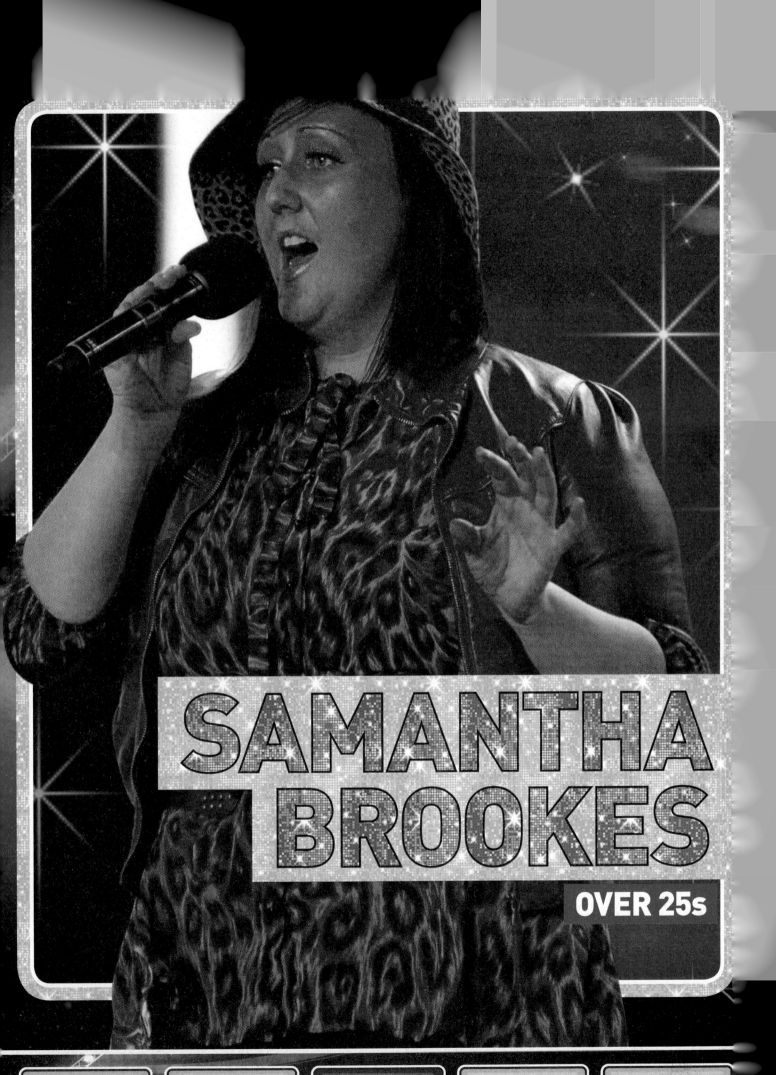

SAMANTHA BROOKES

OVER 25s

WHERE ARE THEY NOW?

It's hard to believe that a whole year has passed since we were cheering for Matt, gasping at Wagner's outlandish performances and wondering if Simon would ever call Storm by his name. So what has happened to the 2010 Finalists in the last twelve months?

Matt Cardle

Week left: Winner   Mentor: Dannii
Audition song: 'I'm No Good'
Performed in 2010 Live Tour: Yes

After the massive excitement of winning *The X Factor*, Matt has had a roller coaster of a year! He received a recording contract and his debut single became the Christmas number one.

He has been working in the studio since the end of *The X Factor* Live Tour, and he's clearly been enjoying every minute. Matt has been co-writing with some hugely talented songwriters, and has loved the chance to challenge himself and learn new skills.

With a number of gigs and TV appearances, his new single 'Run For Your Life' and his first album 'Letters' both set to make a splash in the pop world, Matt is on a glittering high – and long may it continue!

Rebecca Ferguson

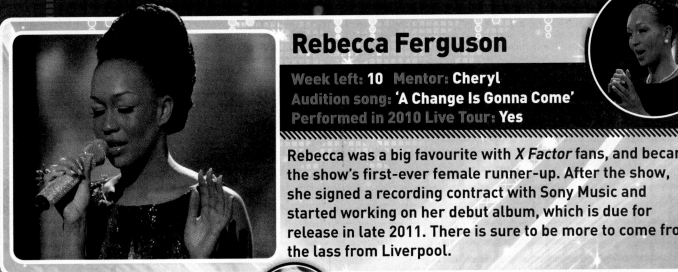

Week left: 10   **Mentor:** Cheryl
Audition song: 'A Change Is Gonna Come'
Performed in 2010 Live Tour: Yes

Rebecca was a big favourite with *X Factor* fans, and became the show's first-ever female runner-up. After the show, she signed a recording contract with Sony Music and started working on her debut album, which is due for release in late 2011. There is sure to be more to come from the lass from Liverpool.

One Direction

Week left: 10   **Mentor:** Simon
Audition song: Band formed at Bootcamp
Performed in 2010 Live Tour: Yes

Niall, Zayn, Liam, Harry and Louis finished the show in third place, but since then their star has been steadily rising. They loved being part of the Live Tour and poured their energy into giving great performances for their fans.

One Direction signed a record deal with Syco Music, and have brought out a book about their experiences, as well as a fabulous debut single, 'What Makes You Beautiful'. It had the biggest pre-order in Sony history, selling 150,000 in the first week, and went to number one.

One Direction are the new ambassadors for Pokémon and have been working hard on their debut album. What will 2012 bring?

Cher Lloyd

Week left: 10   **Mentor:** Cheryl   **Audition song:** 'Turn Your Swag On'
Performed in 2010 Live Tour: Yes

Feisty Cher made a huge impact on the show and was one of the most talked-about contestants of 2010. Although she was voted out in the Semi-Final, she was signed up by Syco Music and started working on her debut album straight away.

Cher's first single 'Swagger Jagger' went in at number one in the UK Singles Chart. Her second single 'With Ur Love' is due for release in October, with her debut album being released the following month. The future's looking exciting for Cher – and the UK can't wait to find out what she's going to do next!

Mary Byrne

Week left: 9 **Mentor:** Louis
Audition song: 'I Who Have Nothing'
Performed in 2010 Live Tour: Yes

Eliminated in the Semi-Final, Mary released a debut single and album – and supported Neil Diamond on tour. There are rumours of a solo concert tour in the future!

Katie Waissel

Week left: 8 **Mentor:** Cheryl
Audition song: 'We Are The Champions' / 'At Last'
Performed in 2010 Live Tour: Yes

Katie is now in a new band and is hard at work promoting their music. Watch this space, guys!

Wagner

Week left: 8 **Mentor:** Louis
Audition song: 'Indigo'
Performed in 2010 Live Tour: Yes

No one can guess what Wagner might do next, but look out for a radio show and more TV appearances!

Paije Richardson

Week left: 7 **Mentor:** Dannii
Audition song: 'Fly Me To The Moon' / 'Man's World'
Performed in 2010 Live Tour: Yes

Paije has stayed focused on his musical career and has been busy gigging. He's promised that his songs will be out soon.

Aiden Grimshaw

Week left: 6 **Mentor:** Dannii
Audition song: 'Gold Digger' / 'Toxic' / 'That's Life'
Performed in 2010 Live Tour: Yes

Since he left *The X Factor*, Aiden has been developing his singing skills and writing music. He has lots of gigs planned so keep an eye on Twitter.

Treyc Cohen

Week left: 5 **Mentor:** Cheryl
Audition song: 'You Got The Love'
Performed in 2010 Live Tour: No

Treyc has been busy treading the boards – she's starred in the West Yorkshire Playhouse's production of *The Wiz*.

Belle Amie

Week left: 4 **Mentor:** Simon
Audition song: Band formed at Bootcamp
Performed in 2010 Live Tour: No

The Belle Amie girls have signed a record deal and released a debut single.

John Adeleye

Week left: 3 **Mentor:** Louis
Audition song: 'You Are So Beautiful'
Performed in 2010 Live Tour: No

John is still writing music and has released a charity single for Project Waterfall.

Storm Lee

Week left: 2 **Mentor:** Louis
Audition song: 'Every Breath You Take' / 'Still Haven't Found What I'm Looking For'
Performed in 2010 Live Tour: No

Following his time on the show, Storm re-released his album 'Soulfillapopkilla' and remains focused on his goal of stardom.

Diva Fever

Week left: 2 **Mentor:** Simon
Audition song: 'Proud Mary'
Performed in 2010 Live Tour: No

Diva Fever brought a huge dollop of fun and colour to the show. They have promised that a debut single is on its way!

Nicolo Festa

Week left: 1 **Mentor:** Dannii
Audition song: 'A Song For You'
Performed in 2010 Live Tour: No

Although he left early, Nicolo hasn't given up on his dream and has promised that he has more music on the way.

F.Y.D.

Week left: 1 **Mentor:** Simon
Audition song: 'Where Did Our Love Go' / 'She Said'
Performed in 2010 Live Tour: No

The boys are following their dream, working hard on writing their own music and gigging.

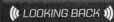

LOOK BACK:

LIVE TOUR 2011

The 2011 Live Tour was the biggest UK arena tour of the year, and both audiences and performers had a fantastic time. Hundreds of thousands of people turned up to watch their fave *X Factor* stars. If you weren't lucky enough to be one of them, here's a taster of the fun they had!

One Direction's Louis went onstage dressed as a carrot and raised over £1,000 for the charity Help for Heroes.

Matt gave a polished performance.

RUNNING ORDER: ACT 1

	ARTIST	SONG
1	CHER	369 / GET YOUR FREAK ON
2	PAIJE	I'M A BELIEVER / HEY YA
3	AIDEN	DIAMONDS ARE FOREVER
4	WAGNER	SHE BANGS / LOVE SHACK
5	MARY	COULD IT BE MAGIC
6	KATIE	HELP
7	CHER	GIRLFRIEND
8	PAIJE	KILLING ME SOFTLY
9	REBECCA	SHOW ME LOVE
10	REBECCA	MAKE YOU FEEL MY LOVE
11	ONE DIRECTION	ONLY GIRL (IN THE WORLD)
12	ONE DIRECTION	GRENADE
13	ONE DIRECTION	KIDS IN AMERICA
	INTERVAL	INTERVAL

RUNNING ORDER: ACT 2

	ARTIST	SONG
14	REBECCA	SWEET DREAMS
15	CHER	STAY
16	KATIE	I WANNA BE LIKE YOU
17	CHER	BOOM SHAKE / WHIP MY HAIR
18	MARY	IT'S A MAN'S MAN'S WORLD
19	WAGNER	SPICE UP YOUR LIFE / LA VIDA LOCA
20	AIDEN	MAD WORLD
21	REBECCA	LIKE A STAR
22	ONE DIRECTION	MY LIFE WOULD SUCK WITHOUT YOU
23	ONE DIRECTION	FOREVER YOUNG
24	MATT	FIREWORK
25	MATT	NIGHTS IN WHITE SATIN
26	MATT	THE WAY YOU ARE
27	MATT	THE FIRST TIME EVER I SAW YOUR FACE
28	MATT PLAY OFF	WHEN WE COLLIDE
29	ALL ARTISTS	HEROES

BACKSTAGE EXCLUSIVE

Choreographer Elizabeth Honan worked with all the acts on the Live Tour, and enjoyed every minute! But who were her favourites?

"I loved working with Cher," says Elizabeth. "She had a great attitude and I enjoyed putting together the big dance routines. Matt Cardle's performances were much more intimate and simple. With him it was all about the voice. I loved the One Direction lads for their sheer ability to get the girls going absolutely crazy!"

Prankster Harry Styles loved playing tricks on the other performers.

Cher brimmed with energy and charisma..

Rebecca brought sheer class to the evening.

Love was in the air when Rebecca and Zayn got together on The X Factor Live Tour.

DON'T MISS
THE 2012 LIVE TOUR

THE X FACTOR
LIVE 2012
TOUR DATES

Manchester	25th February
Liverpool	27th February
Nottingham	29th February
London	4th March
Dublin	6th March
Belfast	9th March
Aberdeen	13th March
Glasgow	17th March
Newcastle	19th March
Sheffield	21st March
Birmingham	25th March
Brighton	26th March
London, The O2	31st March
Cardiff	3rd April

For tickets please visit: xfactor.itv.com/2011/live-tour

Hysterical girls screamed through One Direction's set!

GREAT VALUE STOCKING FILLERS

CHILDREN'S ANNUALS 2012

There's a whole range of fantastic value Pedigree Annuals for both boys and girls! Each one is packed full of great stories, profiles and activities from your favourite brands. Hours of quality entertainment for kids' of all ages!

FAMILY ANNUALS 2012

This range is aimed at the whole family with popular TV series such as Family Guy and South Park, football action in the Shoot Ultimate Book; plus stories, recipes and lots more in the Yours Yearbook. A great stocking filler for mums, dads, bigger brothers, sisters and anyone else you can think of!

Family Guy Annual 2012

South Park Annual 2012

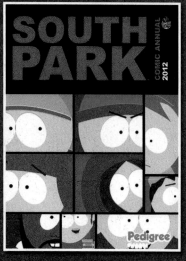

The Ultimate Book Of Football 2012

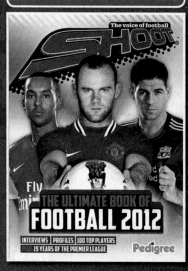

A Year With Yours 2012

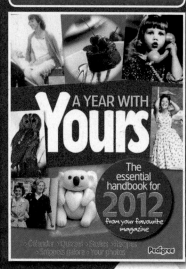

Pedigree®